The Life and Times of
RICHARD I

OVERLEAF LEFT *Chronicle of Petrus de Eboli*,
showing Richard I in Germany. Above, he is
arrested by Leopold's soldiers. Below, he
kneels at the feet of Emperor Henry VI,
asking for forgiveness.
RIGHT Tile from Chertsey Abbey, Surrey,
showing Richard I on horseback.

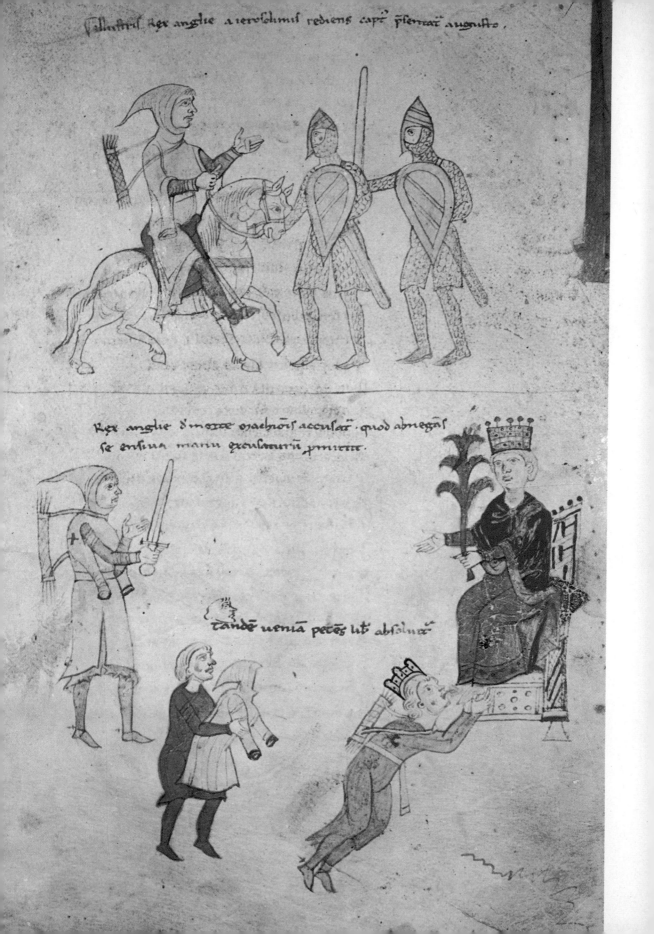

Ilustris rex anglie a ierosolimis rediens capt̄ p̄ferrat̄ augusto.

Rex anglie d̄ morte onachois accusat̄ . quod abnegas̄
se onsina manu oculsar̄u p̄mititr

tande venia peteo lit̄ absolut̄

The Life and Times of
RICHARD I

John Gillingham

Introduction by Antonia Fraser

Weidenfeld and Nicolson
5 Winsley Street London W1

Series design by Paul Watkins
Layout by Margaret Downing

Filmset by Keyspools Limited, Golborne, Lancashire
Printed in Great Britain by
C. Tinling & Co. Ltd, London and Prescot

Introduction

For most of us, Richard the Lionheart has been ensconced since childhood in a pantheon which includes King Arthur, Robin Hood and other legendary – if not mythical – figures: and as a 'folk hero', in John Gillingham's apt phrase, it is unlikely that he will ever be dislodged. It is all the more curious that this basic interest has been accompanied by very little knowledge of the King's actual personality, beyond the bare facts of disappearance on a Crusade, cruel imprisonment and rescue – with the help, perhaps, of the minstrel Blondel – followed by a dramatic return to his own country to confound his usurping brother John. Curious indeed, for the actual history of the reign of King Richard I in no way lets down the legend, and provides a story to equal the most gripping tale of Sir Walter Scott, *Ivanhoe* or *The Talisman*.

The story begins in the rich, strange world of twelfth-century Europe. The Angevin Empire stretched across England and part of France under its King, Henry II and his heiress-bride, Eleanor of Aquitaine. As one of the warring sons of this fascinating if strident couple, Richard's early years were spent half against the chivalrous background of his mother's Court, half campaigning in the nexus of inter-family battles. The fall of Jerusalem at the hands of the 'infidel' preceded Richard's succession to the crown by only a couple of years; by 1189 he was King of England and by 1190 on his way to the Holy Land in that remarkable endeavour, semi-feudal, semi-religious, wholly adventurous, known as the Third Crusade. The extraordinary events leading to the re-establishment of European dominions overseas – 'Outremer', live again in this book, as do the chief characters, including Saladin, the great Muslim general, and Duke Leopold of Austria: it was the symbolic insult given to the Duke's standard which was to prove later such a fatal gesture in view of Richard's incarceration at his hands.

Above all, the true character of Richard himself emerges, physically every inch the noble figure of our romantic imagination with his powerful build, striking red-gold hair and blue eyes, but at no point a mere dummy. Like many another heroic figure he failed in his ultimate objective, in this case to recapture Jerusalem, the Holy City; although by the end of his scant ten years' reign, he had managed to win back much of his own Angevin Empire. John Gillingham sees in Richard I an interesting contrast: a cautious and calculating general on the one hand, as his military successes prove, and a 'risk-taking' individual on the other, destined as a result to die untimely at the age of forty-one. It was also typical of the man that he forgave his assassin before his death. In short it was as a twelfth-century Christian prince that Richard shone, not as a romantic hero; at the same time this able and compelling biography amply demonstrates, with its picture not only of a man but of an age of tournaments and troubadours, crusades and castles, that the two were not really so far apart after all.

Antonia Fraser

Acknowledgments

Photographs and illustrations were supplied by or are reproduced by kind permission of the following (numbers in italic indicate colour illustrations):

Aerofilms: 154–5; Ampliaciones Mas: 19, 94, *112*, 142; Archiv für Kunst und Geschichte: 27, 82, 164–5, 173, 180; Archives Nationales, Paris: 33; Archives Photographiques, Paris: 191–2; Bibliothèque Municipale, Boulogne-sur-Mer: 162; Bibliothèque Municipale, Cambrai: 138; Bibliothèque Nationale, Paris: 38 *(below)*, *77*, 92–3, 107, 123, 126–7, 144, 157; Bodleian Library: 26 *(left centre, left below and right)*, 31; British Museum: *3*, *15*, 20, 24, 25, 36–7, 38 *(above)*, 44, 50, *65 (above)*, 68, 71, 74, 95, *109*, 128, 129, 135, 140–1, 161, 186, *193*, 194, 202 *(below)*, *205, 208*, 215; Burgerbibliothek, Bern: *2*, 78, 79, 182, 183; Casa Aguilar, Barcelona: 142; by permission of the Master and Fellows of Corpus Christi College, Cambridge: *14*, 58, 59, *65 (below)*, 70, 89, 98, 99, 106, 137, 163, 169, 202 *(above)*; Courtauld Institute: 58, 59, 70, 98, 106, 137, 169; Cyprus Tourism Information Bureau: 103; Robert Descharnes: 62–3, 83; Geoffrey Drury: 30; Durham Cathedral Library: 75 *(below right)*; Foto Marburg: 49; Freer Gallery of Art and L. A. Mayer Memorial Association: 151; June Gillingham: 176; Giraudon: 33, 60, 126–7, 138; Green Studio: 210 *(right)*; Michael Holford: 47, *196*; A. F. Kersting: *97*, 102, 166–7; Mansell Collection: 84, 146; Middle East Archive: 39, 40, *100*, 152; Musée de l'Armée, Paris: 130, 131; Musée diocesain, Arras: 114; Musée du Mans: 16; National Monuments Record: 53, 198; Osterrische National-bibliothek: 41, 199, 201; Pierpont Morgan Library: 66; Public Record Office: 54–5; Radio Times Hulton Picture Library: 13, 26 *(left above)*, 61, 85, 120; Jean Roubier: 46, 210 *(left)*; Scala: 206; Staatsbibliothek, Bamberg: 67; Topkapi Palace Museum, Istanbul: 148–9; Trinity College, Cambridge: 75 *(above)*, 75 *(below left)*; Trinity College, Dublin: 210 *(right)*; Ullstein Bilderdienst: 110, 118; Universitat-bibliothek, Heidelberg: 170, 178, 179; University Library, Cambridge: 195; Victoria and Albert Museum: 134; Dean and Chapter of Westminster: 203; Derrick Witty: *80*.

Picture research by Andrea Nelki.

Maps drawn by Design Practioners Limited.

1 Fathers and Sons
1157-87

No other king of England ever caught the imagination of his age as did Richard Cœur de Lion. Troubadour, knight-adventurer, war-lord, Crusader-king – he was all of these things. He was a son who rebelled against the old king, his father. He was a captain who could meet the great Saladin on equal terms, who could conquer Cyprus in a few short weeks. He was a diplomat who built coalitions on a European scale. He was a king held captive by his mortal enemies while a fellow-Crusader invaded his lands and his own treacherous brother tried to snatch his kingdom from him. He was a warrior who lived all his life at the centre of the political stage only to die in an obscure sideshow in a place no one had ever heard of. Although he could not speak English and was not interested in England, he was the first king since the Norman Conquest to become an English folk-hero. Ultimately his name became entangled with that of Robin Hood for, of all English kings, he was the one who fitted most naturally into the world of ballad and legend. But it was not just in England that Richard became a name to conjure with. In thirteenth-century France he could be described as 'the greatest of all Christian kings'. In Syria his name was invoked when Muslim women wanted to stop their children crying: 'Hush child, or the King of England will come.' So far as they were concerned, there was only one King of England, Richard Cœur de Lion.

But, behind the legend, who was Richard? It is the task of historians to tell us this, to strip away the romantic nonsense and uncover the real man. How then, do the historians of the last hundred years see Richard? The great nineteenth-century historian Bishop Stubbs wrote: 'He was a bad king ... his ambition was that of a mere warrior. He would fight for anything whatever, but he would sell everything that was worth fighting for.' More widely read was the judgment of J.R. Green: 'He was at heart a statesman, cool and patient in the execution of his plans as he was bold in their conception.' A French historian of the Crusades, R. Grousset, wrote simply that he was brutal and unintelligent. On the other hand a post-war English medievalist, F. Barlow, described Richard as 'a great man, perhaps too great a man ... shrewd in politics and also capable of diplomacy on a grand scale. More generous than his father, nobler, more imaginative ...'. Finally there is the

Richardus. I.

Cy sensit les ordonances du sa
cre au roy richard dangleterre ·
Chappitre  ·lxxviii·

Ces choses ainsi fait
tes et les apparaulx
apprestes le duc ri
chard vint a londres ou estoient as
sambles archeue sques euesques
ducs contes barons cheualliers et
bourgois le premier dimenche de
septembre pour estre au couron
nement richard duch de normedie
La maniere comment il fut cou
ronne est telle. Cest assauoir pre
mierement vindrent a lencontre
de lui archeuesques et euesques
en grant nombre auecq eulx grant
quantite de noble clergie abbes

et autres en chappes de draps dor
brodees de perles deuant lesquelz
estoient portees croix moult riches
et chieryes et chandeliers auecquez
encenssiers dor et dargent moult
richement ouurez Et en cest es
tat alerent iusquez a la chambre
ou estoit le duch qui ce iour deuo
estre couronne Si le prindrent
et menerent a westmonstier
deuant le grant autel de leglise
Et deuant le duch aloient clers
reuestus comme dit est qui por
toient croix encenssiers et eaue
benoite puis venoient conuentz
chappitres et collettes · Apres ve
noient euesques abbes et ceulx
qui auoient dignites ou millieu

LEFT Coronation procession of Richard I, from Jean de Wavrin's *Chronique d'Angleterre*, produced for Edward IV in Bruges in the late fifteenth century. Richard is depicted walking beneath a canopy flanked by the two Archbishops and preceded by his treasure chest and by a lord carrying his crown.

RIGHT The frontispiece to an order for the coronation of an English king, from an *Apocalypse* written in the mid-fourteenth century and presented to St Augustine's Abbey Church, Canterbury. This shows the king, crowned and enthroned, holding his sceptre and orb.

Enamel of Geoffrey of
Anjou, Richard I's
paternal grandfather, from
his tomb in Le Mans
Cathedral.

verdict of a man who himself wanted to be both statesman and historian: Winston Churchill. 'In politics, a child. The advantages gained for him by military genius were flung away through diplomatic ineptitude. His life was one magnificent parade, which, when ended, left only an empty plain.' What are we to make of such conflicting opinions? It is all very muddling. Perhaps we had better begin again.

Richard was born on 8 September 1157 at Oxford, presumably in the palace of Beaumont. His earliest nourishment is said to have come from the right breast of a nurse whose name was Hodierna. The source which tells us this also says that the left breast was reserved for her own son, Alexander Neckham, who was to grow up to become Abbot of Cirencester and a famous writer. The next twelve years of Richard's life are shrouded in obscurity but he had obviously got off to a good start. Hodierna must have been an excellent nurse; she became a rich and, in her part of the world, a famous woman – she is perhaps the only wet-nurse in history to have a place named after her: the Wiltshire parish of Knoyle Hodierne.

Richard's father was Henry II, King of England, Duke of Normandy, Count of Anjou and, in the right of his wife, Duke of Aquitaine – lord of an empire which stretched from the Scottish border to the Pyrenees. It is conventionally called the Angevin Empire and the name is important. The heart of the empire was Anjou, not England. In historical atlases the Angevin Empire, like the nineteenth-century British Empire, is often coloured red, but this is misleading. It was not the first British Empire. Henry II was born at Le Mans, died at Chinon and was buried at Fontevrault. His son Richard happened to be born in England, but this country awoke no chord in his heart. Shortly before he died, Richard made arrangements for the disposal of his body. His brain was to be buried in the abbey of Charroux (Poitou) and his heart in Rouen (Normandy), while his embalmed corpse was to lie at the feet of his father in the abbey church of Fontevrault (Anjou). For England there was nothing.

England, of course, had its uses. It brought its ruler a royal crown and, above all, it brought him money. The countryside was prosperous and, to all appearances, its prosperity grew with each succeeding decade. There were a few new developments

17

in technology. For example, although water had been harnessed to mills for centuries, the first known windmill in England dates only from the 1180s. But the economic expansion of the twelfth century seems to have been linked with a population increase rather than with technological progress. A population increase meant more hands at work, more stomachs to fill and bodies to clothe, a greater emphasis on production for the market rather than for home consumption, and a more rapid circulation of wealth. By 1200 the total population of England was perhaps between two and three million; there is so little evidence available that we simply cannot compile more accurate statistics. In the twelfth century we are still in the Dark Ages of Economic History. To the modern reader the figures of two to three million may seem remarkably low, but we have to remember that large areas of forest were still needed to provide wood for fuel and building materials (instead of coal, oil, natural gas, iron and steel); that a good deal of land was given over to sheep so that the people could wear woollen clothes (instead of imported cotton and artificial fibres); and that the oxen and horses which provided the most advanced forms of land transport also required grazing land. Above all, we have to remember that in those days an acre of agricultural land produced only a fraction of modern yields.

But however low the yields were, it is clear that in the twelfth century the total acreage under the plough was steadily being expanded. Wheat, rye, oats, barley, peas and beans were grown in fields fertilised by animal dung. Grain grown in East Anglia and the south-eastern counties was exported to Norway and to the densely populated Low Countries. At the same time, however, the number of English vineyards was declining as the growers gave way before the competition of the superior wines from Bordeaux, then a part of the Angevin Empire. English pastoral farmers kept cattle, goats, pigs and sheep – above all, sheep. The fine quality wool grown on the backs of English sheep was in great demand all over Europe, and particularly in the conveniently close industrial towns of Flanders, Bruges, Ghent, Ypres, St Omer, Arras and Douai. The export of wool ensured that England had a favourable balance of trade throughout the Middle Ages. It was said at the time that the wool of England amounted to half the value of the whole land. When a poet from Artois wrote of 'carrying wool to England' this was the medieval version of 'carrying coals to Newcastle'.

With the increasing volume of trade, towns grew in size and number. In the second half of the twelfth century, more than thirty new towns were founded in England. By modern standards, of course, the towns were ludicrously small. London, for example, may have had a population of no more than 20,000 at this date, but it was probably at least twice the size of its nearest rivals, York and Bristol. Thirteenth-century city ordinances dealt with the rearing of cattle in the houses of London, and pigs roamed its streets. Most of the houses were built of wood, though efforts were made to counter the danger of fire by ordering that wood should be replaced by stone and thatch by tiles. According to William Fitzstephen, who wrote a description of the city in Henry II's reign, 'the only plagues of London are the immoderate drinking of fools and the frequency of fires'. It has been observed that the smallest liquor measure in the civic records was a quart. As the towns grew in wealth so their leading burgesses grew in confidence and began to demand municipal self-government.

In general, making due allowance for regional variations, these basic economic and social trends were common to all of Western Europe. The remarkable thing about England,

The baling and shipping of wool, England's most important export in the twelfth century. These two illustrations are taken from a chronicle of the life of Alfonso X of Castile.

even in the twelfth century, was the high level of taxation. The Anglo-Saxon kings before 1066 and after them the Norman kings, had built up a tax system which ensured that an unusually high proportion of the country's wealth found its way into the royal coffers. Naturally the ministers of Henry II and Richard I took good care that their masters were among those who benefited most from the twelfth-century economic expansion. Thus Henry and Richard came to look upon England as a bank from which they could draw all the money they needed. But although banks are important, essential even, they are not the kind of place in which most people want to spend their whole life. They are rather dull places and, except for ambitious civil servants, England in the twelfth century was a rather dull place too. It is hard to know why this should have been so. Perhaps it had something to do with the fact that the overwhelming bulk of the population spoke English, while ever since 1066 the mother-tongue of the ruling classes had been Norman French. Whatever the reason, it remains true that all the really exciting things, in war, in religion, in intellectual life, in literature, in sport, happened abroad, and especially in that part of the world which we call France and was then called Gaul. (In the twelfth century France was the name given to a much smaller region, the lands ruled directly by the kings of the Capetian dynasty.)

In theory the Capetian kings of France were overlords of the whole of Gaul, but many of the princes of Gaul were, in practice, at least as powerful as the king. In legal terms these princes

Plaster cast of the Great Seal of Henry II.

20

were the king's vassals; they were his men (*hommes*) and they owed him homage. In the ceremony of homage the inferior put his hands together, and then placed them between the hands of the superior. By this act he recognised the latter as his lord. It is thought that the modern position of the hands in prayer derives from the ritual of homage, and that previously when men prayed they did so with their arms stretched out wide. The most powerful of the princes who did homage to the king of France – at this time King Louis VII – was Henry II, but we must remember that he owed homage only for his Continental dominions. In his role as king of England he was the independent equal of the king of France.

At the time of Richard's birth, Henry II had been King of England for only three years. He was still a vigorous young man dressed in the latest Continental fashions, like the short cloak which gave him the name of Henry Curtmantle. Everywhere he went, Henry was greeted with enthusiasm as the King who had brought peace and plenty after the civil wars of Stephen's reign (1135–54), the nineteen troubled years when men said that Christ and his saints slept. Even the magnates, the great feudal barons, welcomed the end of strife. Since the basis of their wealth and therefore of their power lay in their estates and the estates of their tenants, they had no wish to see them laid waste by war. Peace at home enabled Henry to think of expansion abroad. By 1157 he had already recovered Northumberland, Westmorland and Cumberland – shires which had been held by the King of the Scots since 1136. He was now planning to conquer Ireland and, in the far South, to extend his lordship over the county of Toulouse. Merely to hold together an empire of this size was a difficult and exhausting task. In order to ensure that his subjects were in the habit of carrying out his instructions, a king had to visit them as often as possible. It was sometimes useful to arrive when they were not expecting to see him. This meant that he had to lead a life of non-stop movement, riding hard from one corner of his dominions to another. Henry II travelled so fast that he seemed to be everywhere at once. Peter of Blois, who was one of the King's secretaries, reported that in a day he would sometimes ride four or five times a normal day's journey. Despite the rumour that he could fly, this meant that he had to be in the saddle so much that he suffered from sore legs. His followers suffered too. This is how Peter of Blois described the problems faced by those who had to try to keep pace with Henry II's unexpected movements:

> If the king has promised to remain in a place for a day – and particularly if he has announced his intention publicly by the mouth of a herald – he is sure to upset all the arrangements by departing early in the morning. As a result you see men dashing around as if they were mad, beating their packhorses, running their carts into one another – in short giving a lively imitation of Hell. If, on the other hand, the king orders an early start, he is certain to change his mind, and you can take it for granted that he will sleep until midday. Then you will see the packhorses loaded and waiting, the courtiers dozing, traders fretting, and everyone grumbling. People go to ask the maids and the doorkeepers what the king's plans are, for they are the only people likely to know the secrets of the court. Many a time when the king was sleeping a message would be passed from his chamber about the city or town he planned to go to, and although there was nothing certain about it, it would rouse us all up. After hanging about aimlessly for so long we would be comforted by the prospect of good lodgings. This would produce such a clatter of horse and foot that all Hell seemed let loose. But when our courtiers had gone ahead almost the whole day's ride, the king would turn aside to some other place where he had, it might be, just a single house with accommodation for himself and no one else. I hardly dare say it, but I believe that in truth he took a delight in seeing what a fix he puts us in. After wandering some three or four miles in an unknown wood, and often in the dark, we thought ourselves lucky if we stumbled upon some filthy little hovel. There was often a sharp and bitter argument about a mere hut, and swords were drawn for possession of lodgings that pigs would have shunned.

To be one of the King's servants was often frustrating, but it was also hectic and exciting and to those who served him well Henry II held out the promise of great rewards. On the whole, he had capable and reliable ministers. Of the men he picked to serve him only Thomas Becket turned out, in the end, to be a disastrous mistake. In his dealings with his own family, however, Henry failed to show the same good judgment: 'A man's enemies are the men of his own house' (Micah 7: 6).

Richard's father was a great King, but his mother, Eleanor

'A man's enemies are the men of his own house'

22

of Aquitaine, was the more fascinating person. She haunted the
dreams of poets and song-writers:

> Were the world all mine
> From the sea to the Rhine
> I'd give all away
> If the English Queen
> Would be mine for a day.

Throughout her life Eleanor had been surrounded by an aura
of romance and scandalous rumour. For fourteen years she had
been married to Louis VII of France – a simple and gentle
man – and she had borne him two daughters. But she complained that he was more like a monk than a king. Then in
March 1152 she and Louis separated; the Church declared that
they were too closely related to each other for it to be a true
marriage. Less than two months later she married a man who
was equally closely related to her, Henry of Anjou and Normandy. (He did not become King of England until Stephen
died in 1154.) There was every reason for speed. Eleanor's
husband, whoever he was, would be the new Lord of Aquitaine.
Already, two landless younger sons had tried to kidnap and
marry her in the hope of obtaining this great inheritance. So
Eleanor urgently needed a powerful protector. Even so, there
were many people who were shocked by the wedding. Not,
it should be emphasised, because she was nearly thirty while he
was only eighteen. When marriages were made for diplomatic
and dynastic reasons this kind of disparity in age was common-
place. They were shocked because Henry was Louis VII's
vassal, and owed him homage for Anjou and Normandy. But
now he was that awkward customer, the vassal who was much
stronger than his lord, and – to add insult to injury – he had
achieved this position by marrying his lord's former wife. It
was no way for a vassal to treat his lord and it created a very
difficult legal and political situation. Nonetheless Henry and
Eleanor prospered. In fourteen years she had never borne a male
heir to the throne of France, but now, in the first six years of
her second marriage, she had five children, four of them boys:
William, who died very young, Henry, Richard and Geoffrey.
Henry II, it was clear, was no monk. Altogether they had eight
children, the last of whom, John, was born in 1167.

23

LEFT Thomas Becket was first Henry II's chancellor and then his Archbishop of Canterbury. Henry had hoped by this move to have a primate who would subordinate Church interests to those of the State. The choice proved disastrous for Becket refused to be the King's tool, and open conflict broke out at the Council of Woodstock in 1163. This illustration from a fourteenth-century chronicle of the *History of England* shows Henry II and Becket quarrelling, while Henry's soldiers look on.

Louis VII had waited two years before marrying his second wife – Constance of Castile – in 1154. She, too, bore only girls and then died in 1160. The need for a male heir to the throne of France was now desperate and it took Louis only five weeks to find a third wife, Adela of Champagne. Eventually, in August 1165, a son was born. The mood of the Parisians, when they heard the news for which they had been waiting so long, was recorded by a young Welshman living in a rented room on the Ile de la Cité. The fame of Peter Abelard had made Paris the centre of the intellectual world, the Mecca of all students. (It was to be many years before Oxford could offer similar facilities.) So Gerald of Wales went to study in Paris and there, on a warm summer's night, he was abruptly awoken when all the bells of the city began to peal. Through his window he could see the flickering light of many flames. His first thought was that Paris was on fire and he rushed to the window. But the fires were bonfires and the bells told not of danger but of joy. The narrow streets were crowded and it was not long before Gerald had discovered the cause of this exultant bedlam. 'By the grace of God there is born to us this night a king who shall

OPPOSITE Becket fled to France in November 1164 and from there he issued constant demands that the King should submit to him. In 1170 a reconciliation took place at Fréteval and the Archbishop returned to his see. He was murdered by four of Henry's knights while at prayer in Canterbury Cathedral on 29 December 1170. Reginald Fitzurse is shown in the illustration striking the fatal blow.

25

The Courts of Chivalry

Richard I was brought up at the Court of his mother, Eleanor of Aquitaine, at Poitiers. At Eleanor's Court, themes of chivalry and courtly love were developed and elaborated by minstrels and troubadours. Taking as their basis the heroes of romantic legend, such as the paladins of Charlemagne or the knights of King Arthur, they evolved a code of love and loyalty to women, where the rituals had to be observed no less punctiliously than the rules of war and the tournament. Women were not regarded as mere servants and chattels of their fathers and husbands, but as creatures worthy of high regard, with virtues and identities of their own.

RIGHT
The troubadour Bernard of Ventadour, who served first at the Court of Ebles III of Ventadour and then at the Court of Eleanor of Aquitaine, before her marriage to Henry II.
FAR RIGHT Adenez, King of the Minstrels, presenting his poem *Diomades* to the Queen of France and the young Countess of Artois. From a thirteenth-century French manuscript.

LEFT ABOVE AND BELOW Two initials from an English Gallican psalter of the early part of the thirteenth century, written at St Augustine's Abbey, Canterbury. The initial 'C' shows musicians playing a harp and a wind instrument, and the initial 'D' shows a man playing a rebec. (Bodleian Ms Ashmol. 1525 fs 79v and 101.)

RIGHT Detail from a twelfth-century manuscript showing David and a servant playing a psaltery and chimebells. (Bodleian Ms Auct. D. f. 88.)

n non de dieu   Mais ce me fait reconforter

le creatour   Q́ me daignierent gmander

q̀ nour duint   Que ceste estoire entendisse

psa grāt doucour   ⁊ a riuer lentrepreisse

Qŀeſames li   .ij. dames enau maint la flour

puiſſons rendre   De ſens de biaute de valour

inrai arimouer   Leur nous ne vuel en apt dire

entendre   Carleurpaiſam ⁊ dout leurire

Je qui fil dogier le danois   Sique bien fai quele morroie

⁊ de bertam qui fu ou lois   De duel ſe fait ne dit auoie

be a hammer to the king of the English.' The newborn boy was given the name of Philip. In the course of time he and Richard became mortal enemies.

At the Court of the king of the English there was now less cause for celebration. After John's birth in 1167, Henry and Eleanor drifted apart. Henry drifted towards the most famous of his mistresses, Rosamund Clifford – 'Fair Rosamund'. Eleanor established a Court of her own at Poitiers, the traditional capital of the dukes of Aquitaine (who were also counts of Poitou). Richard went with his mother and was brought up in an atmosphere very different from that which prevailed in England and Normandy where his father, 'the King of the North Wind', held sway. At Poitiers there were troubadours and tournaments, there was talk of chivalry and courtly love. It was in this society that a new attitude to women was born – an attitude which eventually led to the notion of 'women and children first' and to the odd spectacle of a husband dutifully carrying his wife's shopping basket. In Provençal poetry we can find the new idea that sexual love between men and women was a noble passion and that women, because they could inspire this emotion, were creatures worthy of high regard. What had hitherto been exclusively a man's world, a world in which the women who were most respected were those who possessed the 'male' virtues of courage, wisdom and loyalty, now became a world in which poets said that women should be loved because they were different from men. It should, however, be emphasised that for a very long time to come husbands and fathers proved singularly impervious to this new literary fashion. They continued to regard their wives and daughters as instruments by which property was transferred from one family to another, just as Aquitaine was transferred from the Capetians to the Angevins.

In June 1172, Richard was formally installed as Duke of Aquitaine in ceremonies at Poitiers and Limoges; he was now fourteen years old. Of his life up to this point we know almost nothing. It is clear, however, that he had been well educated. Both his parents were, in their very different ways, patrons of literature and learning. Just as American intellectuals were attracted to the White House in the Kennedy era, so too European intellectuals gathered at the Court of Henry II. In the

28

words of Peter of Blois, 'With Henry of England there is school every day, constant conversation of the best scholars and discussion of controversial questions.' Here men took for granted the twelfth-century cliché that an uneducated king was like an ass with a crown on its head. It is an indication of the change that was coming over Europe – the movement known as the twelfth-century Renaissance – that in the eleventh century such a remark would have been a statement of revolution. Richard was a product of this new environment. He was capable of writing verse in French and Provençal. He could speak Latin well enough to crack a Latin joke at the expense of a less learned Archbishop of Canterbury. He enjoyed music. When the clerks of the royal chapel were singing in choir, he would often walk among them, urging them, with voice and hand, to sing with greater gusto.

He also learned how to be a knight – how to ride and fight on horse-back. He took part in war games called tournaments. The twelfth-century tournament was very different from the formalised jousting of the later Middle Ages which film-makers have made so familiar to us. In Richard's day it was serious training for war as well as a splendid social occasion. In war, battles were won by knights who had learned to fight together as a unit, not by displays of individual prowess. Therefore tournaments were mock-battles contested by teams of knights and, as in war, the more knights in your team the more likely you were to win. If one knight became separated from the rest of his team he might find five or six of his opponents all bearing down on him at once. It was thought extremely clever tactics when one team pretended not to be taking part in a tournament, but then joined in late in the day when all the other knights were exhausted. As in war, if you were captured, you lost your horse and armour to the victorious knight and you might have to pay a ransom as well. Thus a landless younger son could win fortune as well as fame if he became a tournament champion. The classic example of this is William Marshal, the fourth son of a Wiltshire baron. The story of his successsful career on the tournament field was told in an early thirteenth-century poem, *L'Histoire de Guillaume le Maréchal*. As the widely acclaimed expert on knightly affairs he became tutor in chivalry to Henry II's eldest son, Henry. Eventually he married the

William Marshal, the acknowledged expert on knightly affairs of his day, who became tutor in chivalry to the young King Henry. Detail from his tomb in the Temple Church in London.

heiress to the earldom of Pembroke and ended his days as Regent of England during the minority of Henry III (1216–19).

Infantry could also play a part in tournaments. As in war, you could use them as a screen behind which your knights waited until they were ready to charge. In these circumstances tournament fields had to be as big as battlegrounds. They might well cover several square miles. When Richard was a young man there was a tournament about once a fortnight on the Continent; in damp and dreary England there were none at all.

Henry II, like the Pope, did not approve of them. They were undoubtedly a threat to public order. As can be imagined, they very easily developed into hot-tempered battles fought in deadly earnest; moreover, when barons and knights gathered in arms, who could tell what conspiracies and rebellions might not follow? But when Richard became King he encouraged tournaments in England. He knew their value as training for war and he did not fear rebellion.

It was Richard's elder and more frivolous brother, Henry, who was the real tournament enthusiast of the family. Richard was not the kind of boy to take a war game as seriously as war itself. At the age of sixteen Richard had his first taste of war – and his first enemy was his father. It came about like this. Henry II had decided that after his death the bulk of his dominions should go to his eldest surviving son, Henry. In 1170 Henry was crowned by the Archbishop of York – much to the fury of the exiled Archbishop of Canterbury, Thomas Becket – and was known thereafter as the Young King. But Eleanor's duchy was to go to Richard, while the third son, Geoffrey, was to marry the heiress of Brittany. In 1169, as part of this family settlement, Richard had done homage to Louis VII for Aquitaine and had been betrothed to the French King's daughter Alice. Alice was the younger of the two girls born to Louis's second

A tournament mêlée, from *Les Tournois de Chauvency*, written in about 1300. Henri de Blamont, carrying an emblazoned shield, fights with an unknown noble, while other horsemen struggle in the background. (Bodleian Ms Douce 308 c f. 131)

wife, Constance. The elder sister, Margaret, was already married to Henry, the Young King. The basic trouble with this arrangement was that Henry II was still only in his thirties and had no intention of allowing his young sons to govern for themselves. He would give them titles but no authority. For them it was a very frustrating situation. In addition they had cause to fear that, sooner or later, Henry II would decide to provide for his youngest and best loved son, John, at their expense. The split between their parents meant that whenever they needed support against their father they could always turn to their mother. In March 1173, the Young King fled from Henry's Court and went to Paris where he was warmly welcomed by his father-in-law, Louis VII. Early that summer he was joined by Richard and Geoffrey. Eleanor dressed herself up in a man's clothes and rode for Paris too, but she was captured by one of Henry's patrols. She remained her husband's prisoner for the rest of his reign. In May 1174 Richard, having been dubbed a knight by Louis VII, took command of his first serious campaign. He was able to seize the town of Saintes, but quickly lost it again to his father's forces. The Old King, thanks to his speed of movement, powers of organisation and greater cash resources, soon proved himself master of the situation, and in early September two of his rebel sons gave up the struggle. But Richard fought on until his father himself marched into Poitou. Richard would make war on his father's armies but not on his father in person. He submitted. 'Weeping, he fell to the ground at his father's feet and begged forgiveness.'

Having pardoned him, the Old King at once found a use for Richard's rapidly maturing military talents. Henry II had insisted that the castles belonging to the rebel barons of Aquitaine should either be reduced to the state they were in before the outbreak of hostilities or be entirely razed to the ground. Naturally the barons resisted and Richard, with financial help from his father, was given the task of bringing them to heel. He began to learn the difficult art of siege warfare. This kept him busy for the next few years, but they were productive years. The unstable political situation and the enormous number of hill-top castles made Aquitaine a hard school of warfare, but anyone who could survive the course was going to be a master of the art. In 1179, after an arduous apprenticeship,

The Great Seal of Philip Augustus, who succeeded to the French throne as a fifteen-year-old boy in 1180. He was to prove Richard's principal enemy in European affairs.

Richard produced his masterpiece. He laid siege to Taillebourg, a fortified town so well protected by ramparts and natural defences that it was regarded as impregnable. But within a fortnight Richard had taken this 'virgin fortress'. The remaining rebels were so dismayed by this overwhelming demonstration of the young Duke's skill and determination that they at once laid down their arms. Richard was now a famous man.

His elder brother did not find this easy to bear. By comparison with Richard, he had achieved nothing. He was jealous of Richard and angry with his father. The Old King, he felt, had never given him a chance to do well. So once again, in 1182, Henry fled to the French Court. In an attempt to bring him back to the fold, Henry II assured him that Richard and Geoffrey would do homage to him. It took all the Old King's powers of persuasion to make Richard agree to this, but then the young Henry pressed too far. He demanded more than homage; he required that Richard should also swear on some holy relic that he would be faithful to him. This clear proof that his brother

33

did not trust him was too much for Richard. In a white heat of passion he left the Court, having done no homage and sworn no oath, claiming that Aquitaine came to him from his mother and was not his brother's business. Now Henry II was angry too and he ordered Henry and Geoffrey to subdue their brother's pride. To do this they formed a league with those barons who were chafing against Richard's stern rule. Henry II had hoped to curb the independence of his second son, but he did not want to see a general rising of the vassals in the southern half of the Angevin Empire. He tried to call a halt, but Henry and Geoffrey would no longer listen. By the spring of 1183, the rôles were reversed. It was now they who were the rebels against their father while Henry II and Richard fought side by side. Then, in June 1183, a sudden attack of dysentery changed the entire situation. The Young King died, leaving Richard as the heir to the throne.

Three years earlier the heir to another throne had entered upon his inheritance. The new king of France, Philip II – generally known as Philip Augustus – was a very different man from his father, the mild-mannered Louis VII. Although only fifteen at the time of Louis's death in September 1180, he soon showed himself to be a shrewd and unscrupulous politician. While still a boy, he found his life's work. One day at a council meeting of his barons, he sat apart, chewing a hazel twig and apparently lost to the world. When challenged to say what was on his mind, he replied that he had been wondering whether it would ever be given to him to make France great again, as it had been in the days of Charlemagne. To fulfil this ambition he had to destroy the Angevin Empire, and this he set out to do by every means at his disposal, however despicable. He was a singularly unattractive man, a hypochondriac and a coward, but he outlived his enemies and he made France a powerful kingdom. Though nothing like as great a man as Saladin, he was to be Richard's most ruthless opponent.

In 1184 Richard first crossed swords with the man who was to be King Philip's most valuable ally: John, the youngest of the Angevin brothers. Henry II had hoped that now that Richard was the heir to the rest of the empire he would hand Aquitaine over to John. This Richard refused to do. He had spent the formative years of his life in Aquitaine, bending the recalcitrant province to his will, and he was not going to give it up. Once again the Old King set sons against son, but John and his ally Geoffrey were no match for the conqueror of Taillebourg and the victor in a score of skirmishes. Richard kept his duchy. John remained 'John Lackland'.

By this time, Philip Augustus was old enough to begin his favourite game of persuading the Angevins to destroy each other. Not that they needed much persuasion. In a chamber in the palace of Winchester, a fresco, painted according to the Old King's instructions, depicted an eagle being attacked by its four offspring. One of the fledgling birds had gone already; a second went in 1186 when Geoffrey died as a result of a tournament accident. He had been beaten to the ground and then trampled to death by the horse's hooves. But there were still two eaglets left and one of these, John, was portrayed in the act of pecking out the parent bird's eyes. In this situation, Philip's technique was to negotiate with each separately and then reveal to one or more of the others whatever he thought would create the most distrust between them. The way he treated the question of Richard's marriage is a good illustration of his methods. Alice, Philip's half-sister and, for more than fifteen years, Richard's fiancée, was still in Henry's custody; indeed it was rumoured that the Old King had seduced her. Philip, negotiating with Henry, insisted that it was high time the wedding took place. Henry, in reply, proposed that she should marry John instead and that he should do homage to Philip for all the Angevin possessions except England and Normandy, which Richard would retain. At any rate, Philip told Richard that this is what Henry had proposed and, as a result, Richard went off to Paris in 1187 and let the world know that he and the French King were close associates. 'Every day they ate at the same table and from the same dishes; at night they shared a room.' The Old King was dismayed by the reports of this sudden friendship and begged Richard to return. Eventually father and son were reconciled, but while Henry doted on John, relations between the Old King and his heir could not be other than watchful and suspicious. It had begun to look as though Richard's whole life would be dominated by these interminable family squabbles, but then, in the summer of 1187, he heard news which changed his world.

'Every day they ate at the same table'

2
Taking
the
Cross
1187-90

ABOVE Two Knights
Templars or Poor Knights
of Christ and of the
Temple, one of the great
military orders founded in
the twelfth century.

PREVIOUS PAGES
A battle scene, from a
mid-thirteenth-century
*Roman de Girard de
Roussillon*, one of the
knights of Charlemagne.
According to legend,
Charlemagne went on
Crusade to Jerusalem; he
did not, but since he was
the ideal medieval King,
it was thought that he must
also have been a Crusader.

T HE NEWS WAS BAD. Jerusalem had been captured by the
Infidel and an apparently flourishing Christian kingdom was
tottering on the brink of total ruin. During the night of 3–4
July 1187 the army of Jerusalem had camped on a hill at Hattin,
a few miles west of the Sea of Galilee. The Christian soldiers
spent a miserable and sleepless night, their eyes smarting from
the smoke which blew into their camp as the enemy systemati-
cally set fire to the dry scrub which was all that grew in this
waterless region. When morning came the King of Jerusalem,
Guy of Lusignan, could see what he must have known already.
His army was completely surrounded by a far greater Turkish
force. Inspired by the presence of their most sacred relic, the
Holy Cross, the Christian soldiers put up a tremendous fight.
But the outcome of the battle was a foregone conclusion: the
army of Jerusalem was destroyed, and Guy of Lusignan and the
Holy Cross were captured. Those Templars and Hospitallers
who managed to survive the battle were executed immediately
after it. As the elite-troops of the Christian army, these monk-
knights could not be allowed to live to fight another day. With
practically all its fighting men either killed or captured, the
kingdom of the Franks – as the Muslims called the Christians
who lived in the East – lay helpless at the feet of the invader.
In an attempt to appease the wrath of God and save Jerusalem
itself, the defenders of the Holy City indulged in extraordinary

ABOVE The site of the Battle of Hattin, where, in 1187, the army of Jerusalem was utterly destroyed by Saladin, and its leader, Guy of Lusignan, was captured. In the distance can be seen 'the Horns of Hattin'.

LEFT *Chronicle of Godfrey de Bouillon*, one of the leaders of the First Crusade. This version, produced in France *c.* 1187, shows Crusaders setting off for Jerusalem.

rituals of penance. Mothers shaved the heads of their daughters and then made them undress to take cold baths in public on the Hill of Calvary. It was in vain. On 2 October, the anniversary of Mahomet's ascent to heaven from Jerusalem, the Muslim army marched into the Holy City. The al-Aqsa mosque was restored to Islam. But it is symptomatic of the greater tolerance of the Muslims that the Jewish community was allowed to return to Jerusalem and four Christian priests were allowed to hold services in the Church of the Holy Sepulchre. Ever since 1099 when the first Crusaders captured the Holy City and massacred the people who lived there, the Christians had always treated Jerusalem as though it belonged to them alone.

Guy of Lusignan had been beaten by a greater man. The Muslim leader was Al-Malik al-Nasir Salah ed-Din Yusuf; in

ABOVE The silver-domed
Al-Aqsa Mosque in
Jerusalem, which was
built by the Fatamid
Caliph, Al-Zahir, in 1034.
When Jerusalem was
captured by the
Crusaders, the Mosque
became the headquarters
of the Order of Knights
Templars.

OPPOSITE Twelfth-
century ground-plan of
the Church of the Holy
Sepulchre in Jerusalem.

the West he was known as Saladin. He came from a family of
Kurdish army officers and from 1152 he served in the household
of Nur ed-Din, the ruler of Muslim Syria. For years he seemed
to be just another young officer, distinguished only by his skill
at polo. He accompanied his uncle, Shirkuh, when the latter
was sent to Egypt by Nur ed-Din. In 1169 he succeeded his
uncle as Vizier of Egypt, and in the next few years the young
officer became a great statesman. When Nur ed-Din died in
1174, it was Saladin who married his widow and took over his
rôle as the champion of Muslim Orthodoxy and as the pro-
tagonist of the Holy War against the Christian intruders.
Saladin was borne up by the unshakeable conviction that he
was destined to unite the world of Islam and drive the Christians

40

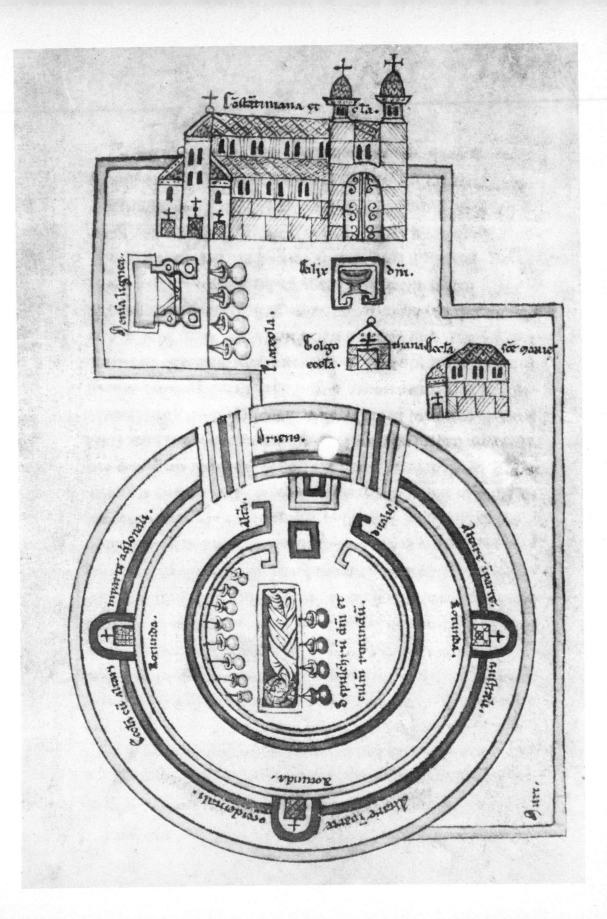

out of the Middle East. He wanted all Muslims to recognise his moral leadership as well as his political overlordship. Thus in his dealings with friend and foe Saladin was unusually generous and honest. He probably broke fewer promises than any other successful politician. It was these moral qualities which made Saladin a legendary figure, a man admired even by his enemies in the West.

By the end of 1187 only three coastal towns, Tyre, Tripoli and Antioch, were left in Christian hands. Inland a handful of castles still held out. Many garrisons had surrendered quickly because they knew they could rely on Saladin to keep his word to spare their lives. Outremer – 'the land beyond the sea' – was on the verge of extinction, less than a hundred years after the men of the First Crusade had called it into life. Since the failure of the Second Crusade in 1148, the knights of Western Europe had been relatively reluctant to go East, but the news of the disaster at Hattin and the fall of Jerusalem changed all that. In November 1187 Richard took the Cross. When a man took the vow to go on Crusade he was handed a piece of material cut in the shape of a cross. It was intended that this should be sewn onto his surcoat. North of the Alps, Richard was the first prince to take the Cross in this manner. Characteristically he acted in haste, without seeking his father's permission. Not until January 1188 did the Kings of England and France take the Cross. Neither was keen to go on Crusade – as long ago as 1172 Henry had promised to mount a Crusade and ever since then he had done nothing about it. But now the reluctant Kings were swept along by the tide of public opinion. In every way possible, preachers and troubadours stirred up enthusiasm. Men who did not take the Cross received gifts of a distaff and wool, implying that they were no better than women. According to Muslim reports, the preachers used visual aids: 'Among other things they made a picture showing the Messiah, and an Arab striking Him, showing blood on the face of Christ – blessings on Him! – and they said to the crowds: "this is the Messiah, struck by Mahomet the prophet of the Muslims, who has wounded and killed Him".' In another picture,

Jerusalem was painted showing the Church of the Resurrection with the Messiah's tomb. Above the tomb there was a horse, and mounted on it was a Saracen knight who was trampling the tomb, over which his horse was urinating. This picture was sent abroad to markets and meeting places. Priests carried it about, groaning 'Oh, the shame.' In this way they raised a huge army, God alone knows how many.

The rewards offered to those who took the Cross were considerable. On the most mundane level, repayment of any debts they owed was postponed until their return; while they were on Crusade their property was taken under the protection of the Church. More important, they were granted a plenary indulgence which freed them from the terrors of purgatory and hell, and held out to them the promise of eternal life in heaven. In the words of St Bernard of Clairvaux, the most successful saint of the twelfth century, they were being offered an astonishing spiritual bargain.

O mighty soldier, O man of war, you now have a cause for which you can fight without endangering your soul; a cause in which to win is glorious and for which to die is but gain. Or are you a shrewd businessman, a man quick to see the profits of this world? If you are, I can offer you a splendid bargain. Do not miss this opportunity. Take the sign of the cross. At once you will have indulgence for all the sins which you confess with a contrite heart. It does not cost you much to buy and if you wear it with humility you will find that it is worth the kingdom of heaven.

'A cause in which to win is glorious and for which to die is but gain'

Richard, of course, enjoyed war, and no war could bring greater prestige to the warrior than the war against the Saracens, the war in the Holy Land, the centre of the Christian world. On this battle-ground no act of bravery, no chivalrous deed, would go unnoticed. But it would be a mistake to think that Richard was indifferent to religion and to the attractions of a plenary indulgence. One of the King's clerks, Roger of Howden, recorded two occasions – in 1190 in Messina and in 1195 in France – on which Richard went through a religious and emotional crisis. On both occasions the pattern was the same. First came a profound awareness of the sinfulness of his life; in 1195 this occurred when an illness followed close upon a warning he had received from a hermit. 'Be thou mindful of the destruction of Sodom and abstain from what is unlawful; for, if thou dost not, God's vengeance shall overtake thee.' Second,

43

an abject confession; at Messina he threw himself, naked and holding three scourges in his hands, to the ground at the feet of a group of prelates. Finally there came the performance of penance and the attempt to lead a better life. In 1195 this meant many things. It meant regular attendance at morning church – and not leaving until the service was over; it meant distributing alms to the poor. It also meant avoiding unlawful intercourse; instead he was to sleep with his wife, Berengaria, something which he had apparently not done for a long time. Partly in view of this and the fact that his wife bore him no children in eight years of marriage, it has become fashionable to say that he was a homosexual. It is, of course, possible and the hermit's reference to Sodom is certainly suggestive. It cannot however, be proved and there is some evidence which suggests that he was quite as much interested in the opposite sex. Among the accusations levelled against him in 1183 by the rebel barons of Aquitaine was the charge that he was in the habit of kidnapping their wives and daughters and then, when he had taken his pleasure, of handing them down to become his soldiers' whores. Naturally it would be naïve to believe everything his enemies said about him. Unquestionably, however, he did acknowledge an illegitimate son and it seems improbable that this was the issue of a homosexual relationship. A man of Richard's temperament, subject to fits of remorse, would be well aware that a Crusade was a religious act as well as a great military adventure. Had not his savage ancestor, Count Fulk the Black, made the pilgrimage to Jerusalem on no less than three occasions? And to a soldier, a Crusade was even better than an unarmed pilgrimage. As the troubadour Pons de Capdeuil put it, 'What more can kings desire than the right to save themselves from hellfire by powerful deeds of arms?'

Crusades required organisation as well as enthusiasm. It was agreed that the men of the King of France should wear red crosses, the men of the King of England white crosses and the men of the Count of Flanders green crosses. Other decrees were issued at Le Mans where Richard had joined his father. These included arrangements for the collection of a crusading tax – the Saladin Tithe – and rules of conduct which the Crusaders were supposed to observe. They were not to swear or gamble, and the only women who were to be allowed on Crusade were

OPPOSITE The Mouth of Hell: the nightmare of the medieval Christian. The illustration is taken from a twelfth-century psalter from St Swithin's Priory, Winchester.

45

washerwomen of good character (for Crusaders were supposed to be neatly dressed). Henry II wrote to the Patriarch of Antioch to say that help would soon be on the way.

Henry was over-optimistic. Once again feuds flared up in Poitou involving Richard. The war spread to the lands of the Count of Toulouse; and when Richard looked to be on the point of capturing Toulouse itself the King of France intervened. He invaded Berri. Henry, in turn, sprang to the defence of his empire. So the summer months went by, while – for all the King knew – the last fragments of the kingdom of Jerusalem might have been lost. Eventually public opinion in the West forced the warring princes to come to a peace conference at Bonmoulins in November 1188. Instead of peace, however, the conference produced a new war. Richard was anxious to go on Crusade as soon as possible but he feared that, if he left before his father, Aquitaine would soon have a Duke called John. During the autumn King Philip had played on this fear. Now

OPPOSITE The kitchens of Fontevrault in the second court of the Abbey. The extraordinary pyramidal structure, known as the Tour d'Evrault, was built in the twelfth century.

BELOW The great Angevin castle of Chinon, Henry II's favourite residence, where he died on 6 July 1189.

Philip and Richard rode together to the conference and presented a joint ultimatum. The wedding of Richard and Alice should be celebrated at once and Henry should publicly acknowledge that Richard was his heir. Henry refused, presumably because he did in fact hope to see Richard supplanted by his younger brother. On hearing the Old King's answer Richard knelt before Philip and did homage to him for all the Angevin lands on the Continent. It was, in effect, a declaration of war. In the interests of the Crusade, the papal legate, sent from Rome, did his best to prevent the war but could do no more than postpone it. In June 1189 Richard and Philip invaded Maine while Henry, now a sick man, withdrew before them, setting fire to Le Mans, the town in which he was born, in order to cover his retreat. Like a wounded animal making for its lair, he headed back to Chinon, the castle of his ancestors. Richard led the hunt so eagerly that he neglected to put on a hauberk. Wearing no armour but his iron cap, he quickly caught up with Henry's heavily-armed and slow-moving rearguard – too quickly perhaps for he only just escaped with his life. The rearguard was led by William Marshal, the former tournament champion and one of the most respected knights of the age. As the Marshal turned to deal with the pursuit, Richard suddenly saw the danger: 'By the legs of God, Marshal, do not kill me! I am not armed.' 'No, I'll not kill you,' retorted William, 'but I hope the Devil may.' Then, adjusting his aim, he ran his lance through Richard's horse. Just ten years later, a similar piece of carelessness was to cost Richard his life.

For the moment, however, fortune favoured Richard, while his father's position deteriorated rapidly. On 4 July Henry was forced to accept a humiliating peace. Among other things he had to promise to grant an amnesty to all who had conspired against him. He asked to see a list of those who needed this pardon. At the top of the list he found John's name. It was the final blow. For John's sake he had driven Richard to rebellion and now John had quietly joined the winning side. Of his sons, only the illegitimate Geoffrey was there to see him through his last hours, brushing away the flies which settled on his face. 'The others are the real bastards.' The Old King had said it before and he had cause to say it again. On 6 July he died at Chinon. From there his body was carried to Fontevrault and

The tomb of Henry II in the choir of the Abbey Church of Fontevrault.

laid in the choir of the abbey church. When Richard arrived at
Fontevrault, he strode directly into the church, saying nothing.
Without showing any sign of emotion he stood for a while at
the head of the bier. Then he turned away. He was King now
and there was work to be done.

He began by praising the loyalty of those who had stayed
with his father to the bitter end. William Marshal, in particular,
was soon high in Richard's favour and was sent to England to
prepare for the arrival of the new King. Queen Eleanor was
released from captivity to govern the country in the meanwhile. On her instructions many of Henry II's other prisoners
were freed, for, as she wrote, she had found 'from her own
experience that prisons were distasteful to men and that to be
released therefrom was a most delightful refreshment of the
spirits'. The result, according to the historian William of
Newburgh, was that 'transgressors were free to transgress more
confidently in the future'.

At Rouen on 20 July Richard was girded with the ducal

loca dñice paſſionis uiſitatur. p̄ter arripuit ſatis magnifice a burgū. cū ſitu p̄ hungariā ꝑ bi apſuit hituruſ. Eodē āno rex t̄ abyſſū ortacie abſor̄ maledixit fuit ſt geniture ſue. apd chinim peti ꝓ paulii die clauſit extremū apud fonte ebraudi poſtqꝫ regnu rxxxiiii. menſibz. vii. diebz. v. Eod ous elyenſis epc. iiij. kl ſept obiit

Coronatio illuſtri reg anglorum Ricardi.

apd weſtmon p̄ſentibz. W. de oſt

sword and invested with the standard of the duchy of Normandy. In August he came to England and had his father's treasure weighed and counted. It amounted to well over one hundred thousand marks, but some twenty-four thousand had to be spent at once in order to buy peace from France. So far as Philip was concerned, Richard was no longer an ally; he had stepped into his father's shoes.

On Sunday 3 September 1189 he was crowned in Westminster Abbey. In their descriptions of the ceremony the writers of the time have given us the first detailed account of a coronation in English history. Along a path made of woollen cloth, Richard was escorted from his chamber in the palace of Westminster as far as the high altar of Westminster Abbey. At the head of the procession went the clergy, carrying holy water, crosses, candles and censors, and chanting as they moved along. First among them were the priors, next the abbots, then the bishops. In the midst of the bishops were four barons carrying four golden candelabra. After them came Godfrey de Lucy carrying the King's Cap of State, John Marshal holding the golden spurs, William Marshal, newly created Earl of Pembroke, with the golden sceptre, William Fitzpatrick, Earl of Salisbury, with the golden verge. Next came three more earls, David of Huntingdon, Robert Blanchemains of Leicester and Richard's own brother John. Each of them bore a golden Sword of State. Then came six barons carrying the royal robes and insignia. The great golden crown, studded with precious stones, was carried by William de Mandeville, Earl of Essex. Richard himself, flanked by two bishops, followed the crown. He was covered over by a silk canopy which was held aloft by four more barons. Behind came the rest of the laity.

On reaching the high altar, Richard took the coronation oath. Kneeling before a copy of the Gospels and the relics of many saints, he swore that all the days of his life he would observe peace, honour and reverence towards God and the Holy Church; that he would exercise right justice over all the people committed to his charge, and that, if any bad laws and evil customs had been introduced into the kingdom, he would abolish them and would enact good laws in their place. Then Richard was anointed. All his clothes were stripped off except his breeches and his shirt, which was bare to the chest. Baldwin,

OPPOSITE Passage from the thirteenth-century *Chronicle of the Kings of England*, describing the coronation of Richard I. The King's head, wearing the crown, is depicted in the margin, and below, Richard is shown with a bishop.

the Archbishop of Canterbury, then anointed him with holy oil on his head, chest and hands. (Until Victoria all subsequent monarchs were anointed in the same way. She was anointed only on the head and hands.) It was this act of anointing which conferred upon the new ruler the divine sanction for his kingship, and it was this, rather than the crowning, which lay at the heart of the coronation service.

> Not all the water in the rough rude sea
> Can wash the balm from an anointed king.

Richard was then dressed in the royal robes, given the Sword of Justice and fitted out with golden spurs. Thus clad, he was led back to the high altar, where the Archbishop adjured him, in the name of Almighty God, not to take the crown unless he genuinely intended to keep the oaths he had sworn. Richard replied that, with God's help, he intended to observe them all. The Archbishop then crowned him. The crown was so heavy that Richard could keep it on his head only when two earls helped to take the weight. Finally, Archbishop Baldwin gave him the sceptre and the verge and Richard mounted the throne. He sat there while Mass was celebrated. During the service a bat was seen to flitter around the throne, and this was odd because it was the middle of the day. There were those who shivered at the sight, looking upon it as an evil omen.

However, the coronation was now drawing to its close. There remained only the procession back to Richard's chamber. Here the King was allowed to change into lighter clothes and a lighter crown. He then sat down to enjoy the coronation banquet. The clergy, in due order of rank, dined at his table, while the laity, earls, barons and knights, had separate tables. The citizens of London served in the cellars while the citizens of Winchester had the honour of looking after the kitchen. All feasted splendidly: some idea of the scale of the affair can be obtained from the fact that at least 1,770 pitchers, 900 cups and 5,050 dishes had been bought for the occasion. The whole occasion was magnificent, just the kind of pageantry in which Richard, unlike his father, delighted. With his powerfully built figure, reddish gold hair and piercing blue eyes he was admirably equipped by nature to play the leading rôle. And there was one part of the otherwise traditional ritual which seems to have been unique to 1189. Normally it was the Archbishop of Canterbury who took the crown from the altar in order to place it on the monarch's head; but this time Richard himself picked up the crown and handed it to the Archbishop. It was a characteristic gesture of self-help.

But at the end of the day it seemed as though the forebodings of the superstitious had been justified. While the feasting continued inside the palace, a riot developed outside. Some Jews, bringing gifts for the new King, had tried to enter the palace, but the Christian crowd at the gates would not have this. They fell upon the Jews, killing some and wounding others. The trouble then spread to the City of London, where it continued throughout the night. Jews were killed, their houses plundered and burned down. Richard was furious because the Jews were under his special protection – not because he was unusually tolerant but because, like all kings of the time, he regarded them as a useful source of revenue. Despite his efforts to prevent them, there were more anti-Jewish riots in the next few months: at Lynn, Norwich, Lincoln, Stamford and elsewhere. Men were full of the crusading spirit. They longed to see Jerusalem and the Holy Cross, and they looked with anger at the descendants of the people who had clamoured for the

Early twelfth-century wall painting from the church of St Michael and All Angels at Copford in Essex. The scene shows the raising of Jairus's daughter and Jairus – as a Jew – is depicted wearing the Jewish cap.

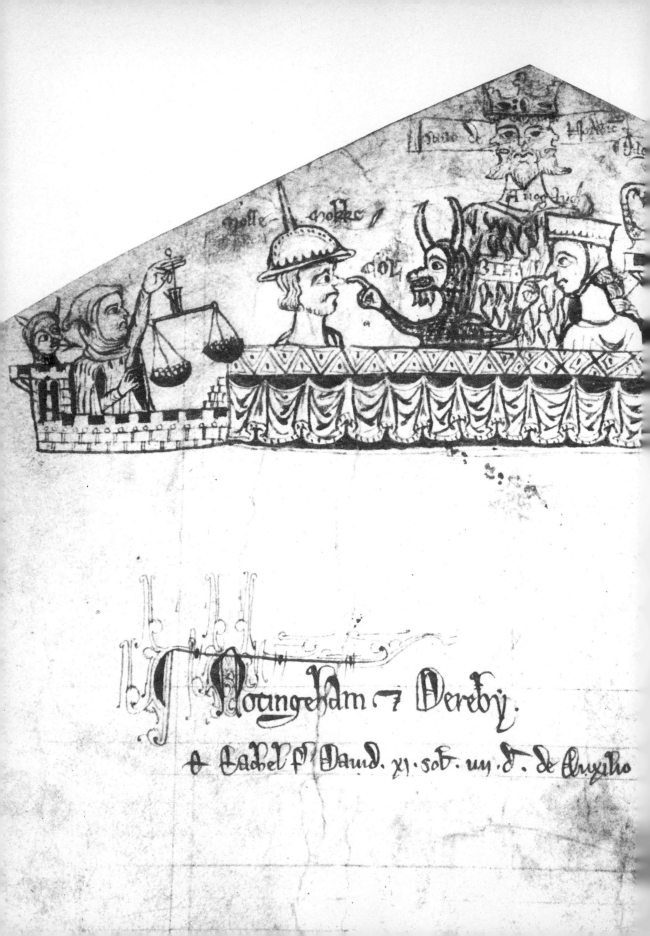

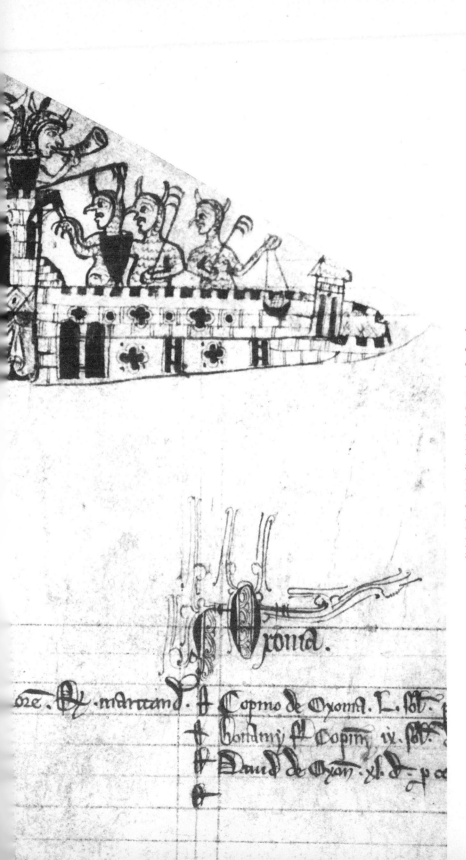

The riots that broke out during Richard I's coronation celebrations were a manifestation of the strong anti-Semitic feelings current in England in the late twelfth century. These feelings are shown in the illustration at the head of an exchequer document recording payments made by Jews to the Crown. The Jews found that they had to pay heavily for the protection – such as it was – afforded them by the King.

crucifixion of Christ. Besides, going on Crusade was an expensive business and the loot taken from Jews could help many a poor but pious man on his way. This wave of popular anti-Semitism reached its height at York in March 1190. About one hundred and fifty Jews managed to escape the mob and take refuge in the castle. But urged on by a fanatical hermit the mob proceeded to besiege the place. When the Jews realised that they could not hold out much longer most of them committed suicide, having first killed their wives and children. The rest, relying on the besiegers' promises that they would be spared if they accepted Christian baptism, came out of the castle and were promptly massacred.

By this time Richard had already left the country. In the words of Sellar and Yeatman in *1066 and All That*, 'Whenever he returned to England he always set out again immediately for the Mediterranean and was therefore known as Richard Gare de Lyon.' He had, in fact, stayed in England only long enough to make the financial arrangements for his Crusade. To this end he sold everything that could be sold, manors, castles, towns, privileges, sheriffdoms and other public offices. All these items were bought and sold in the ordinary, day-to-day business of government, but never had so much come onto the market at the same time. Richard was in a hurry. 'I would sell London,' he is reported to have said, 'if I could find anyone rich enough to buy it.'

He was also faced by an awkward political problem. He was still unmarried and his only child was his illegitimate son, Philip. Should he die on crusade, there was no obvious heir to the throne – and in view of the mortality rate among Crusaders, it was quite likely that he would die. The men who stood nearest to the throne were his brother John and his half-brother the illegitimate Geoffrey. His nephew Arthur, the posthumous son of Geoffrey of Brittany, was still a child. But both John and Geoffrey were ambitious enough to make a bid for the Crown while Richard was away. So he had Geoffrey elected Archbishop of York and forced him to take priest's orders. This automatically made him ineligible for kingship and it was for this very reason that Geoffrey had deliberately avoided being consecrated before, despite the fact that he had been Bishop-elect of Lincoln from 1173 to 1182. Richard also made Geoffrey

'I would sell London if I could find anyone rich enough to buy it'

56

promise to stay out of England for three years. To John Lack-land, Richard granted vast tracts of land, including Nottinghamshire, Derbyshire, Somerset, Dorset, Devon and Cornwall. In addition, he was given the Norman county of Mortain, and he became the Earl of Gloucester by marrying the heiress to the earldom. Richard hoped that this new-found wealth would blunt the edge of his brother's discontent, but just in case it did not, John also was banished for three years.

On 11 December 1189 Richard sailed from Dover. Though he did not know it, it was to be more than three years before he returned to England. He was soon in conference with King Philip. They swore to help each other and defend each other's possessions as though they were their own. On both sides those magnates who were staying at home promised not to attack the territories belonging to the Crusader Kings. Richard and Philip planned to meet at Vézelay on 1 April 1190 so that they might leave together. They were late already. The Emperor and King of Germany, Frederick Barbarossa, had left home six months before. He had chosen the traditional land route to the Holy Land, through the Balkans and the Byzantine Empire. But by the time that the Kings of the West actually did set out from Vézelay – in July 1190 – he was already dead, drowned in a river in Asia Minor. This placed an even greater responsibility on the shoulders of Richard and Philip. They had decided to march south through France and then to take ship for Outremer. Richard assembled a huge fleet from the ports of England, Normandy, Brittany and Aquitaine. He sent it round through the Straits of Gibraltar, planning to meet it at Marseilles. In March 1190 he issued the Chinon ordinances, a set of simple rules for the maintenance of discipline in the fleet:

> Anyone who slays a man on board ship shall be thrown into the sea lashed to the corpse; if on land he shall be buried in the ground tied to the corpse. Anyone convicted by lawful witnesses of striking another so as to draw blood shall lose his hand; but if he strikes with his hand without drawing blood he shall be dipped three times in the sea. Anyone who uses opprobrious, abusive, or blasphemous language against his fellow shall pay on each occasion one ounce of silver. A convicted thief shall be shaved like a champion, tarred and feathered, and put ashore as soon as the ship touches land.

Two details from Matthew Paris's itinerary from London to Jerusalem which he drew up in the mid-thirteenth century.

RIGHT The section from London to Dover, and through the northern part of France. In his drawing of London are marked the Tower, St Paul's, Westminster Abbey and Lambeth and the city gates of Ludgate, Newgate and Cripplegate. Above is the city of Rochester on the Medway, the Abbey at Faversham founded by King Stephen, the Cathedral at Canterbury and Dover Castle.

FAR RIGHT The section through Paris, Troyes and south to Beaune and Chalon.

58

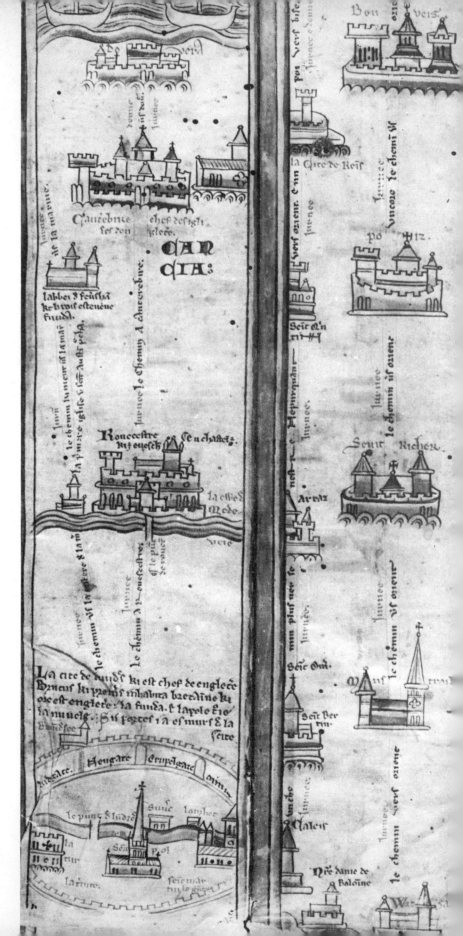

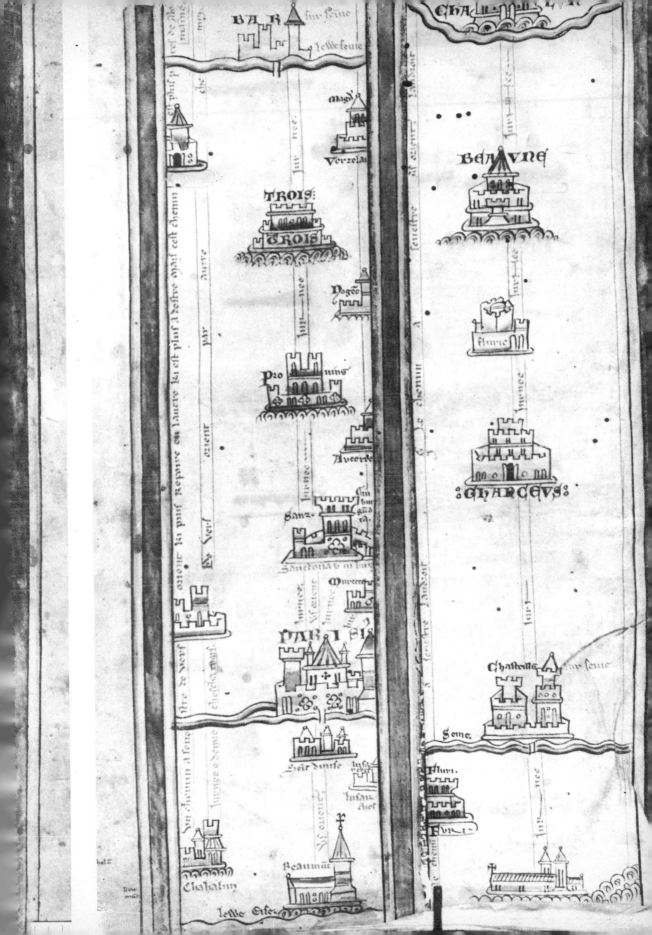

BAR sur seine

CHA

jessesoune

magd

BEAVNE

Verzelai

fluvie

TROIS:

TROIS

Nogee

Prounins

fluvie

Avcerre

CHARCEVS

Sanz

Muerre

PARISIS

Chasteau sur seine

Seine

Seit diuise

fluvi

Chahalu

Beaumo

jessefle

Chahalu

All was ready when the news came that Philip's wife, Queen Isabel, had died on 15 March. This caused yet another delay. It was now almost two and a half years since Richard had taken the Cross; it was beginning to look as though he would never get away. Many Crusaders, impatient of the politics of kings, had already made their own way to Outremer. At last, however, Richard received the staff and scrip which were the traditional attributes of the pilgrim. When he leaned on it, the staff broke. Undaunted by this omen he went to Vézelay and joined forces with Philip. Here the two Kings concluded a vitally important agreement. They were going to war to win land and plunder as well as glory and they decided that the spoils of conquest should be divided equally between them. Then, on 4 July 1190, the third anniversary of the Battle of Hattin, their armies began to move off. The Crusade had begun.

3
Winter in
Sicily
1190-1

Unfortunately there is no way of obtaining an accurate estimate of their numbers. It is clear, nevertheless, that it was a very large army, though we have to remember that in Richard's day this meant no more than a few thousand men. An eye-witness described the camp of the two Kings at Vézelay as a veritable city of tents and pavilions. To us the army would have seemed a small one – and yet there are indications that it was as large as a twelfth-century army could possibly be. The problems involved in feeding thousands of men and horses imposed an upper limit on the size of armies. It has been calculated, for example, that if an army sixty thousand strong took with it provisions to last for one month, it would need about eleven thousand carts. If these carts were stretched out in single file this would mean a supply train well over a hundred miles long. Such a wagon train would be hopelessly vulnerable to enemy raids – and it would be several days before a commander at the head of the column even knew of an attack on the rear. On the other hand, if the army tried to do without a supply train and to live off the country it was limited by the amount of food which the surrounding area could produce. The methods employed by the medieval farmer meant that this was not much. His grain yields per acre were at best only one quarter or one fifth of the yields obtained in the early twentieth century. In these circumstances six thousand rather than sixty thousand was about the maximum size of a twelfth-century army. It is interesting to observe that when Richard and Philip reached Lyons they decided to separate because the countryside was no longer able to provide enough food to support their joint army.

Fortunately for the historian, the army was accompanied by two men who left behind detailed accounts of the Crusade. Even more fortunate is the fact that these two men had very different points of view; we are thus often permitted to see the same events from different angles and can obtain some kind of perspective. One of them was a royal clerk named Roger. Since he was also parson of Howden, a parish in Yorkshire, he is generally known as Roger of Howden. His chronicle is sober and reliable. As a member of Richard's household Roger was very well-informed: he liked to insert copies of any official

PREVIOUS PAGES Detail of one of the twelfth-century capitals from the Benedictine cloister in Monreale.

OPPOSITE ABOVE Making a knight, an illustration from the *Roman de Girard de Roussillon*. Servants place spurs on the new knight's feet, while the king buckles his sword. The knight puts his hands together in homage to the king as his lord.

OPPOSITE BELOW Illustration from Matthew Paris's *Chronica Majora* showing the defeat of the Christians by Saladin at the Battle of Hattin, and the capture of the relics of the True Cross.

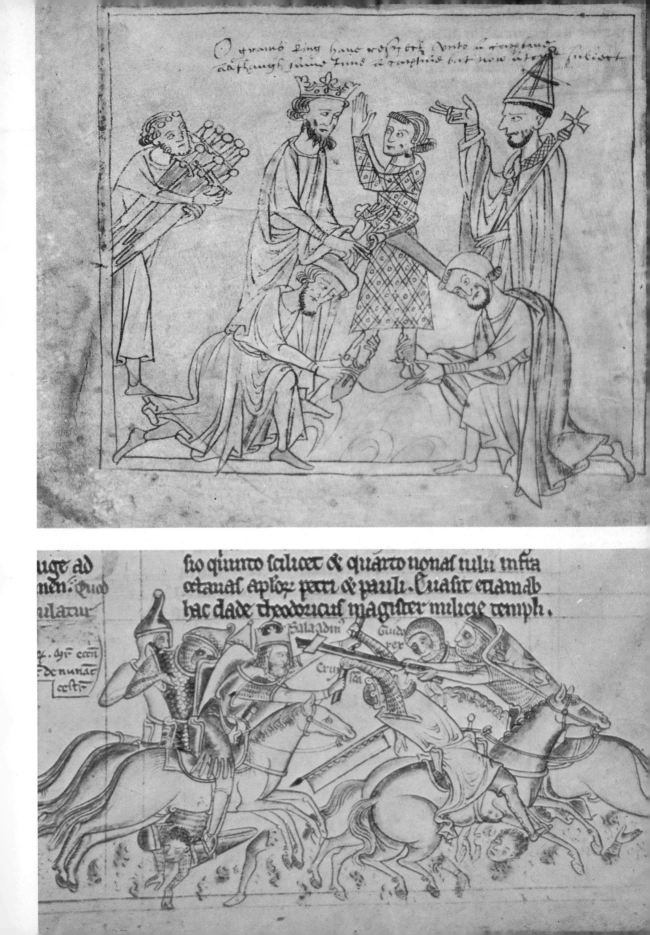

RIGHT The army on the march, from the *Maciescowski Psalter*. The upper section shows baggage carts filled with clothes, armour and kitchen utensils.

OPPOSITE Monks of the Abbey of St Michael, Bamberg with their patron saint; the medallions show operations in the production of a bound codex. From a twelfth-century *Opera* of St Ambrose.

documents, treaties and the like, which came into his possession – and naturally many did. Thus he kept what almost deserves to be called the official diary of the Crusade, at any rate for the period up until August 1191 when he returned home, probably in the company of King Philip of France. But Roger's chronicle is not as dry as most official histories. He was a keen sightseer and he liked to jot down quick descriptions of the places he visited – of Marseilles, for example:

> It is a city situated twenty miles from the mouth of the Rhône and is subject to the king of Aragon. Here can be found the relics of St Lazarus, the brother of St Mary Magdalene and of Martha. After Jesus raised him from the dead he became bishop of Mar-

66

Comment noz gens se mirent
au retour. Et comment les tur

seilles. The city possesses a fine harbour, almost completely enclosed by high hills, but capable of holding many large ships. On one side of the harbour is the cathedral close; on the other the great abbey of St Victor where a hundred Benedictine monks serve God. Here, so they say, are preserved one hundred and forty bodies of the Innocents who were slaughtered for Christ; also the relics of St Victor and his companions, the rods with which Our Lord was scourged, the jaw-bone of St Lazarus and one of the ribs of St Laurence the Martyr.

OPPOSITE
The employment of 'Greek Fire' is shown in this history of William of Tyre.

Moreover, Roger knew that his readers were interested in anything that seemed curious or wonderful. Here, for example, is a characteristic passage:

In the sea around Sardinia and Corsica some very strange fish may be found. They can leap into the air and fly for about a furlong before diving back into the water. One man happened to be sitting at table on board ship when suddenly one of these flying-fish landed on the table right in front of him, so he can vouch for the fact that these odd creatures really do exist. This same area is also inhabited by certain birds of prey which hunt these fish and feed upon them.

The second of our two informants was a Norman minstrel named Ambroise. He composed a long poem entitled the *Estoire de la Guerre Sainte*, 'History of the Holy War'. Ambroise saw things from the point of view of the ordinary soldier. He shows us their dogged courage, and their sufferings; he records their dreams and their disappointments. Whereas Howden takes us into the Council chamber and shows us kings and counts at work, Ambroise takes us into the tents of the poor soldiers and tells us what they thought of the decisions taken by their commanding officers.

At Lyons the crusading army encountered its first setback. The rear of the English army was delayed for three days when the bridge over the Rhône collapsed under the weight of those trying to cross. A hundred or so fell into the river. Mercifully, however, only two were drowned. Not until Richard had organised the building of a bridge of boats could the rest of his army get across. Philip, meanwhile, was on his way to Genoa. For 5,850 silver marks he had hired a Genoese fleet to convoy his army to Outremer.

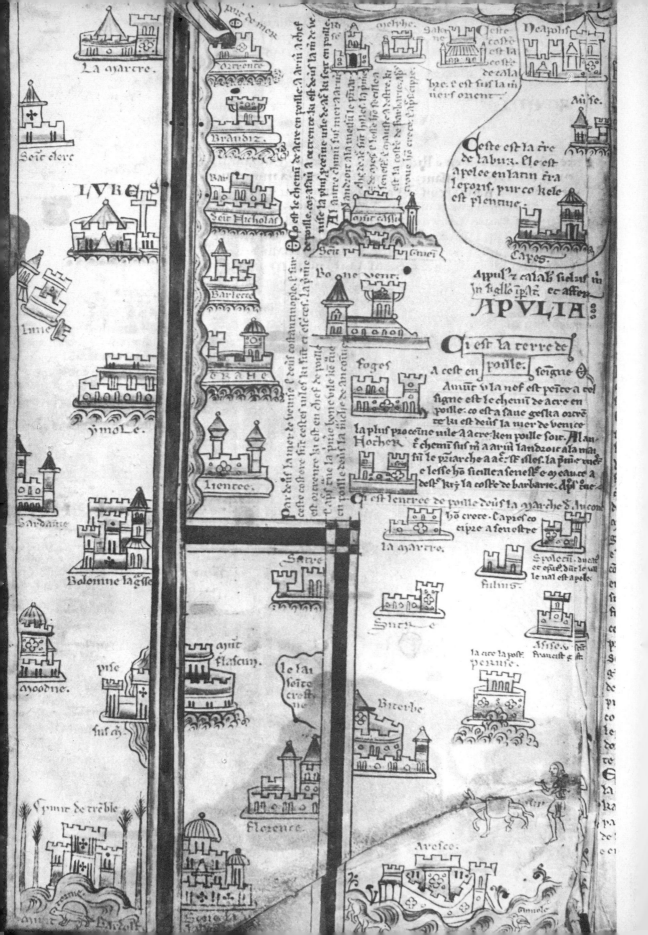

La ajartre.

Seie clere

LVBES

Iunie

ymole.

Sardanne

Bolonne lagsse

ajoodne

prse

sub

Cpmir de treble

Otrente

Brandiz.

Bar

Seir Nicholas

Barlere

Trane

Lientree.

Serre

ajut flaseun.

le fai soire crostine

Florence

pnc de mer

Co el le chemi de acre en poille. A aru a chef de poille. co; aßai a acrenre. ca eß deuß la mer de unfe la plus pceine uile de as ks fer en poille

Al aune chini sus mer a arul landzor ala meßu le priarche a ae. ke ßef. e deiß la coße de barbarie. Aßs et le oice de iiauf. A dext. ku et la coße de barbarie. Aßs poue ha crece. Capscaipe.

Bo one uenr

foges

Hochem

Ci eß lentree de poille deuß la ajarche d'incon

melrhe   Salon ne   Ceite coßte eß la coße de Mal   Neaphs

bze. e eß sus la mi nerf onent

Auße

Ceste eß la cre de labuz. Ele eß apelee en larin cra lepozis, pur co kele eß plenrue.

Capes.

Apulz e catab siclas in in tgello ipsaz. ec affon APVLIA:

Ci eß la terre de
A cest en poille. seigne
Amur ula nof eß poice a cel signe eß le chemi de acre en poille. co eß a saue geska ourre re lu eß deuß la mer de venice la plus pceine uile a acre. ken poille soir. Al au e chemi sus m a arul landzor a la meßu le priarche a ae. ke kles. la pnie mer e leße ho ßiellea seneße e ay cauce a deß krz la coße de barbarie. Aßs eue

ho crece. Capresco eipze a seu oßre

La ajartre

Spoletiu. duens ce oßuek dur le ual le ual eß apele

filius

Snere

Aßke. o ße francesk ß ße

la cre la poße pemße

Biterbe

Areseo.

fumole

On 1 August Richard reached Marseilles, where he expected to find his huge fleet of over one hundred ships waiting for him. The fleet, however, had been held up in Portugal. The King of Portugal had persuaded the sailors to help him in his struggle against the Moors of Spain. Unfortunately once the fighting was over, the sailors turned their attention to the wine and women of Portugal with the result that many of them ended up in gaol. Eventually the fleet commanders were able to negotiate their release, but the upshot of it all was that by the time the fleet reached Marseilles – three weeks late – they found Richard already gone. Some of Richard's troops, led by Archbishop Baldwin of Canterbury, had left with the intention of sailing straight to Tyre, while the King himself, having hired thirty ships from the merchants of Marseilles, had coasted eastwards to Genoa where he found Philip lying ill in a house near the church of St Lawrence. Here the Kings had the first of their many disagreements. Philip asked for the loan of five galleys. Richard offered three, which Philip refused. It was a small matter, but it boded ill for the future of the Crusade.

In leisurely fashion Richard sailed on down the coast of Italy, frequently going ashore to stretch his legs. But although he landed at the mouth of the Tiber, only a few miles from Rome, he did not bother to visit the Pope, Clement III. Indeed a cardinal who was sent to meet him was told in no uncertain terms just what Richard thought of the greed of the Papacy. The gospel preached in Rome was the gospel according to the mark of silver – or so contemporary satirists insisted. It was not that Richard was in too much of a hurry to visit Rome, he made this plain by staying ten days at Naples and five days at Salerno. He had nothing to say to the Pope, but Salerno was the centre of the world of medicine and Richard wanted to talk to the doctors there. Despite his powerful physique, he was constantly troubled by a feverish illness, an ague. According to one contemporary commentator, it was the state of almost continuous trembling to which he was reduced by this illness which goaded Richard into a determination to make the world tremble before him. Whether or not he took the advice of the doctors of Salerno, we do not know. Some of it was worth taking. One of their favourite maxims was 'After breakfast walk a mile; after dinner rest a while.'

ſõ de q̃dam
ep̃o armato
capto a Rege
Ric̃o.

ABOVE Detail from the thirteenth-century *Chronicle of the Kings of England* showing a bishop clad for battle.

OPPOSITE Detail from Matthew Paris's itinerary from London to Jerusalem, showing the route through Italy, including Pisa, Modena and Bologna on the left, Florence in the central part and Arezzo and Viterbo on the right.

While at Salerno, Richard learned that his fleet, after refitting at Marseilles, had reached Sicily and was waiting for him near Messina. So he pushed on and crossed the Straits of Messina between Italy and Sicily on 22 September. Earlier that day he had had a narrow escape. While travelling with just one companion, he was told of a villager who owned a fine hawk. Believing that only noblemen had the right to own hawks, Richard pushed his way into the peasant's house and seized the bird. He was at once surrounded by a crowd of angry villagers and when he refused to give it back they attacked him with sticks and stones. One man drew a knife and Richard struck him a blow with the flat of his sword, only to see it snap off at the hilt. So the Crusader King was reduced to pelting villagers with anything he could lay his hands on in order to make good his escape from a very awkward corner. Nine years later when he was side-tracked into an enterprise almost as trivial as this one there was to be no escape.

That night he slept in a tent on the Sicilian shore. Next day he assembled the whole of his fleet and made a ceremonial entry into the port of Messina. An eye-witness described the scene:

> The populace rushed out eagerly to behold him, crowding along the shore. And lo! on the horizon they saw a fleet of innumerable galleys, and then, far off, they could hear the shrill sound of trumpets. As the galleys came nearer they could see that they were painted in different colours and hung with shields glittering in the sun; they could make out standards and pennons fixed to spearheads and fluttering in the breeze. Around the ships the sea boiled as the oarsmen drove them onwards. Then, with trumpet peals ringing in their ears, the onlookers beheld what they had been waiting for: the King of England, magnificently dressed and standing on a raised platform, so that he could see and be seen.

The pomp and noisy splendour of his arrival stood in marked contrast to the quiet way in which Philip had slipped into the town a week earlier. After disembarking, Richard conferred with Philip, who at once announced his intention of leaving for the Holy Land that same day. But no sooner had the Genoese fleet left the harbour than the wind shifted and, much to his dismay, Philip was forced to return to Messina and to further meetings with the King of England. Philip lodged in a

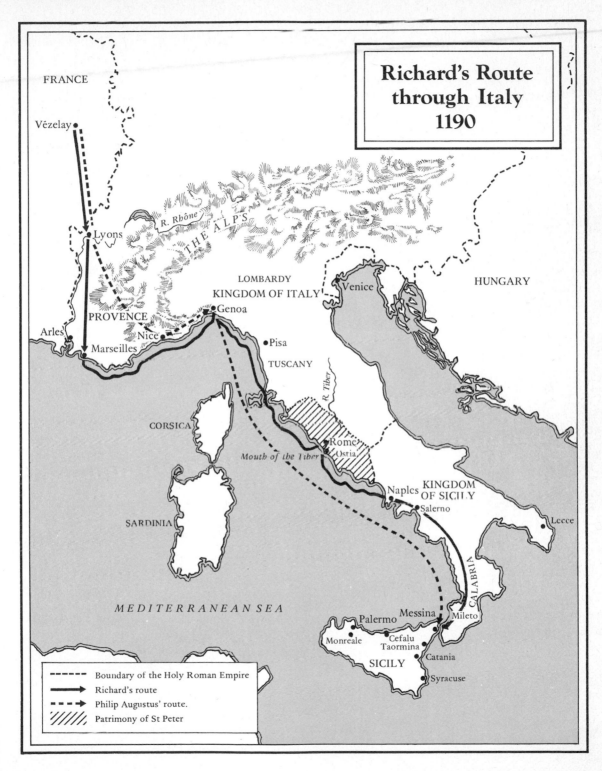

Richard's Route through Italy 1190

FRANCE

Vézelay

Lyons

R. Rhône

THE ALPS

LOMBARDY
KINGDOM OF ITALY

Venice

HUNGARY

PROVENCE

Genoa

Nice

Arles

Marseilles

Pisa

TUSCANY

R. Tiber

CORSICA

Mouth of the Tiber

Rome
Ostia

KINGDOM
OF SICILY

Naples

Salerno

Lecce

SARDINIA

CALABRIA

MEDITERRANEAN SEA

Palermo

Messina

Mileto

Monreale

Cefalu
Taormina

Catania

SICILY

Syracuse

- - - - - Boundary of the Holy Roman Empire
————▶ Richard's route
- - - -▶ Philip Augustus' route.
////// Patrimony of St Peter

Medicine in the Twelfth Century

During his journey through Italy, Richard I visited the city of Salerno, which was the great medical centre for Western Europe. The town had been taken by Normans under Robert Guiscard in 1076 and was at the height of its prosperity in the late twelfth century. Its medical school is said to have been founded by four legendary 'masters' – a Latin, a Greek, a Jew and a Saracen – representing the various influences present in the school.

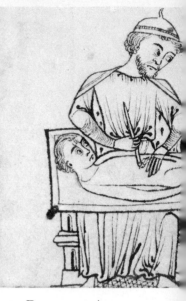

LEFT Doctors treating diseases of the eye and the nose, from a medical treatise, c. 1200.

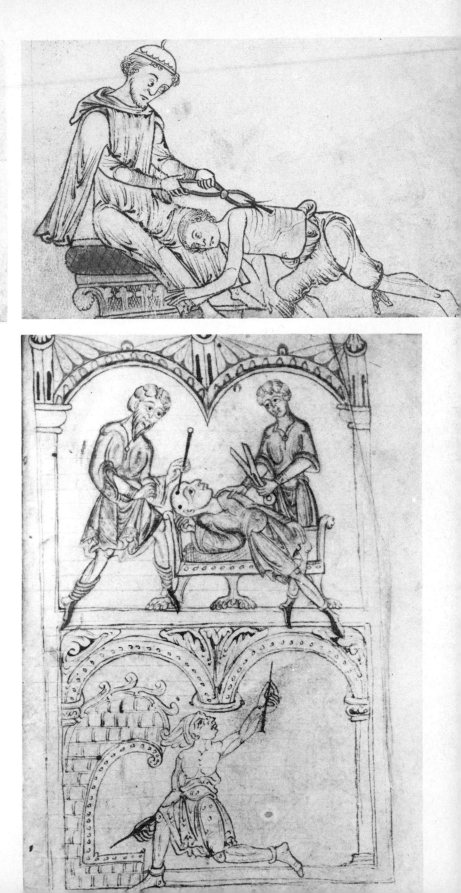

ABOVE Illustrations from an early thirteenth-century medical treatise showing: LEFT an abdominal examination; RIGHT the extraction of an arrow.

RIGHT Cauterising a wound with red-hot instruments which an assistant is heating in the lower part of the drawing. This illustration is taken from one of the medical books given by a doctor, Master Herebert, to the Benedictine Priory in Durham. The book dates from the first part of the twelfth century and it contains the earliest English drawings of patients and doctors.

palace in the city, while Richard and his army camped outside the walls.

Entirely by chance, they had arrived in Sicily at a critical moment in the history of this fascinating country. The twelfth century had been a Golden Age for the kingdom of Sicily – a kingdom which included much of southern Italy as well as the island itself. It was a fertile and prosperous land where the greedy goats had not yet done their work of destruction. Besides corn – for Sicily was one of the great granaries of the Mediterranean world – there were oranges and lemons, cotton and sugar-cane in abundance. It was a land to tempt a conqueror and had already been conquered several times in its turbulent history, most recently by the Normans – cousins of the men who conquered England – in the decades between 1060 and 1090. But the most remarkable thing about Sicily was not its wealth but the diversity of its population. Greek, Arab and Norman lived side by side, each with their own language and religion. The Court at Palermo spoke Norman French and issued decrees in Latin, Greek and Arabic. Yet these very different communities lived together fairly well. The Muslim traveller Ibn Jubayr remarked on the absence of discontent among the island's Muslim population and noted with interest that Christian women were beginning to follow Arab fashions: they wore veils when they went out of doors and they never stopped talking. The blend of different cultures produced a unique civilisation. At Palermo, Monreale and Cefalù the visitor can still see superb examples of its art and architecture.

But in 1190 Sicily stood on the eve of another conquest. Its troubles were brought about by a dispute over the succession to the throne following upon the death of King William II in 1189. He had no children and his heir was his thirty-five-year-old aunt, Constance. But she was married to a German, Henry of Hohenstaufen, the son and heir of the old Emperor Frederick Barbarossa. No one in Sicily wanted a German king and Pope Clement III had a terrifying vision of what would happen to the papacy if it came to be completely surrounded by the territories of one over-mighty ruler. So Pope and Sicilian barons conspired together against Constance and her German husband. The crown passed to Tancred of Lecce, an illegitimate cousin of William II. He was, in the most literal sense of the words, an

OPPOSITE Muslim pilgrims on their way to Mecca, from a manuscript of the Baghdad School.

وَكَادَ يَنْزِعُ الجِمَالَ الشُّمَّ وَالنُّشَدَ

مَا الحَجُّ سِيرَكَ تِأَوُّبًا وَإِدْلَاجًا وَلَا الْعَيَايَا أَجْمَالًا وَأَجْدَالَا

الحَجُّ أَنْ تَقْصِدَ الْبَيْتَ الْحَرَامَ عَلَى تَحْجِيلِ وَلِلْحَجِّ لَا يَبْغِي بِهِ حَاجَا

وَسُطَّى كَأَهْلِ الْإِنْصَافِ مُتَّخِذًا رَدْعَ الْهَوَى هَادِيًا وَالحَوْنَ مِنْهَاجَا

ʃ notarii Greci ʃ Noī Saraceni   ʃ noī latini   bigam̄ nocte scribēs tācred̄.

tācred̄ recipit lr̄as̄ bigam̄

cursor bigam̄   cursor bigam̄   cursor bigam̄

ABOVE The Sicilian Court in the 1190s, showing notaries writing in Greek, Latin and Arabic. At the bottom right, Tancred is depicted receiving a copy of the manuscript.

RIGHT The Capital and Court of Sicily during the reign of Tancred.

ugly little bastard, whose enemies never tired of poking fun at his dwarfish figure. He looked, it was said, like a monkey with a crown on its head. His hold on the throne was anything but secure. He faced a revolt on the island, while on the mainland rebel barons joined forces with an invading German army. No sooner had he overcome these threats than he was faced by the problem of having an enormous army of Crusaders encamped within his unsettled kingdom. They were supposed to be going to Jerusalem but who could tell what damage they might do *en route*? Only a few years later, in 1204, a Crusading army sacked the greatest city in the Christian world, Constantinople, and with that blow destroyed the Byzantine Empire. Tancred was right to be alarmed. Moreover, there were family matters on which Tancred and Richard were far from seeing eye to eye. King William II had been married to Richard's sister Joan. When he died a dower should have been assigned to his widow. But Tancred did not trust her. He kept her in close confinement and withheld the dower. Clearly Richard was not going to stand for this. Immediately after his arrival, he sent envoys to Palermo, and Tancred agreed to release Joan, but without her dower. Moreover William II, in his will, had left a large legacy, including money, gold plate and war galleys, to his father-in-law Henry II. As it happened, however, Henry died a few months before William, so Tancred regarded this part of the will as null and void. Richard took a different view. The bequest had been intended to help finance Henry's Crusade. Now here was Richard, Henry's heir and a Crusader. Naturally he claimed the money and the galleys.

To add to the complications the Crusaders and the – mainly Greek – population of Messina soon took a violent dislike to each other. According to an English chronicle, on the day after his entry into Messina Richard had announced his intention of keeping strict discipline by having gallows erected on which he said he would hang all thieves and trouble-makers irrespective of race. Philip, on the other hand, took no notice of the wrongs done by or against his men. For this reason the Sicilians called one the Lion and the other the Lamb. But not even the grim threat of the gibbet could check the quarrels and skirmishes between Richard's men and the local population. Ambroise blamed the latter:

81

RIGHT The church and cloisters of San Giovanni degli Eremiti, in Palermo, which was built by the Norman King of Sicily Roger II in 1135.
It is an exotic creation showing the mixture of Byzantine and Arab influences – the bell tower and body of the church are surmounted by mosque-like cupolas, while the cloisters have Arab arches.

OPPOSITE The finest Norman monument in northern Sicily is the Benedictine monastery of Monreale. This was begun by William II in 1174 and eight years later the monastery church became the metropolitan cathedral. The beautiful cloisters were completed in 1174 and contain fine sculptured capitals (see pp 62–3) and columns covered in Cosmati work.

For the townsfolk, rabble and the scum
Of the city – bastard Greeks were some,
And some of them Saracen born –
Did heap upon our pilgrims scorn.
Fingers to eyes, they mocked at us
Calling us dogs malodorous.
They did us foulness every day.
Sometimes our pilgrims they did slay,
And their corpses in the privies threw.
And this was proven to be true.

On the other hand, Ambroise did admit that the soldiers were anxious to make friends with the women of Messina, though he adds that they had no intention of seducing them –

LEFT The crowning of William II of Sicily, a mosaic from the interior of Monreale Cathedral, which was begun by William in 1174.

RIGHT Matrix and impression of the Seal of Joan, the sister of Richard I, and Queen of William II of Sicily. After William's death she married Raymond VI, Count of Toulouse.

they merely wanted to irritate their husbands. Almost certainly, rising food prices lay behind all this trouble. The presence of a large army stretched the resources of the region, and prices went up in response to the increased demand. But this is not how the Crusaders saw it. They put the blame on the greed of the local shopkeepers. Soon the Crusaders and the Griffons — as the Greeks were called by the men of the West — were virtually at war. Rather than allow the riots to go on indefinitely, Richard decided, on 4 October, to seize control of Messina. King Philip had tried to make peace between the two sides and he would have no part in so drastic a step. The enthusiasts in the English camp suspected him of having gone over to the Sicilians. When the French prevented Richard's war-galleys from attacking Messina from the sea, the English felt sure that they had been betrayed. But on the landward side, where Richard was directing operations, the Angevin forces had better luck. The gates of the city were broken down and the troops stormed in with Richard at their head. All who resisted were cut down; and it was believed that some townspeople threw themselves from the roofs of their houses rather than fall into the hands of the victors. It was all over so quickly that, in Ambroise's words, it would have taken longer for a priest to say Matins than it took the King of England to capture Messina. After the fighting came the plundering – the natural reward for those who had risked their lives in a good cause. This is how Ambroise described it:

And ye may know of surety
That much was lost of property
When they successfully attacked
The town. It speedily was sacked.
And there were women taken, fair
And excellent and debonair.

When King Philip saw Richard's banners waving above the walls and towers of Messina, he was furious. He demanded that they should be taken down and his own hoisted up in their place. This was not just an empty dispute about whose flags should wave over the town. To plant a banner in a captured town was to stake a claim to the plunder. What Philip wanted was a share of the spoils. True, he had done nothing to deserve it, but he reminded Richard of the agreement they had made in Vézelay. As a temporary arrangement, to last until King Tancred's reaction to the fall of Messina was known, Richard permitted his banner to be hauled down and the city put in charge of the Templars and Hospitallers. But to ensure that he still kept control of the situation, Richard took hostages from among the wealthier citizens of Messina and began to build a wooden castle on a hill overlooking the town. He called the castle Mategriffon, meaning 'check the Greeks'.

If he were to recover Messina, Tancred had very little choice. By 6 October he had agreed terms with Richard. He would pay 20,000 ounces of gold in lieu of Joan's dower. In addition, a marriage was arranged between one of Tancred's daughters and Richard's nephew, Arthur of Brittany, whom Richard designated as his heir should he die without issue. Richard received another 20,000 ounces of gold which he was supposed to settle upon Tancred's daughter when the marriage took place. In return Richard acknowledged that his claims on Tancred had been met in full and promised that for as long as he was in Sicily he would give Tancred military aid against any invader. This clause in the treaty was directed against Henry of Hohenstaufen, now King Henry VI of Germany. (Later, when Richard was in a German prison he was to be reminded of the alliances he had made in Sicily.) As for the citizens of Messina, they were, in theory, to have their property restored.

In an effort to prevent further disturbances, the three Kings fixed the price of bread at a penny a loaf and laid down that no merchant should make a profit of more than ten per cent on a deal. Whether or not this price freeze was rigidly enforced, the Crusaders were in fact able to spend a further six months in Sicily without there being any more serious trouble. Another cause of dissension, this time within the army, was gambling. Philip and Richard therefore banned all gambling by ordinary soldiers and sailors except when their officers were present. Soldiers who disobeyed this order were to be whipped on three successive days, while sailors were to be dipped in the sea three times. Knights and clergy could play for up to twenty shillings a day, on pain of a fine if they exceeded this limit. Kings, however, were specifically permitted to gamble away as much as they pleased. Once more, Philip and Richard agreed to divide equally any conquests they made in the future. But, in the opinion of Richard's followers, this appearance of harmony was deceptive. The French King was envious of Richard's success and beneath a gentle exterior he concealed the cunning of a fox.

By now it was too late in the year to sail safely to the Holy Land so the two Kings decided to winter in Sicily. The time passed quietly and pleasantly enough. In the Holy Land, meanwhile, the Christian army, hemmed in by Saladin, was suffering terribly from disease and starvation. Whenever a horse was killed it was at once surrounded by a crowd of jostling soldiers, each fighting to obtain a piece of the flesh. Whole horses were devoured, head, intestines and all. Men were seen down on their hands and knees, eating grass. In the castle of Mategriffon, outside Messina, Richard celebrated Christmas in magnificent style. King Philip was his guest and all who were there marvelled at the splendour of the gold and silver plate, at the variety and abundance of meat and drink. It was estimated that with a fast, direct passage, a ship could reach the Holy Land from Marseilles in fifteen days. The trip was to take Richard ten months.

While he was in Sicily Richard heard strange stories about a Cistercian abbot who lived as a hermit in Calabria and who was supposed to have the gift of prophecy. This man was called Joachim of Fiore. He believed that he had discovered the concealed meaning of the Bible, and especially of the Book of Revelation. This discovery led him to see a pattern in history,

'I have gone on crusade too soon'

87

a pattern which enabled him to predict the future of the world. Richard was intrigued and asked Joachim to come and talk to him. Joachim came and expounded that prophetic system of thought which has been described as the most influential one known to Europe before the appearance of Marxism. Joachim divided world history into three ages: the Age of the Father, the Age of the Son and the Age of the Spirit. The Third Age was to be the culmination of human history, a time of love, joy and freedom when God would be in the hearts of all men. The Empire and the Church of Rome would have withered away. In their place there would be a community of saints who had no bodily needs, therefore there would be no wealth, no property, no work. Complicated calculations had revealed to Joachim that the Third Age was nigh; it would come some time between 1200 and 1260. What particularly interested Richard was Joachim's identification of Saladin as the sixth of the seven great persecutors of the Church in the Second Age. Joachim prophesied that Saladin would soon be overcome, leaving the way clear for the seventh persecutor. When Richard asked Joachim if he could date the defeat of Saladin, Joachim replied that it would occur seven years after the capture of Jerusalem by the Muslims (i.e. not until 1194). 'In that case,' said Richard, 'I have gone on crusade too soon.' 'Not at all,' answered Joachim, 'Your coming is much needed and the Lord will give you victory over His enemies and will exalt your name above all the princes of the earth.'

After Saladin there would come the seventh persecutor, Anti-Christ, who would rule the world for three and a half years. According to Joachim Anti-Christ was already waiting in the wings ready to make his entrance. He had been born in Rome and would be elected Pope before revealing his true self to the world. This prophecy made Richard wonder whether it was not the present Pope, Clement III, whom he disliked, who was in fact the Anti-Christ. Joachim, however, refused to alter his system to take account of Richard's prejudices. The churchmen in Richard's entourage seem to have been interested, rather than impressed by Joachim's ideas. Most of them, after all, were practical, down-to-earth men chosen by a king who wanted bishops who knew how to command men and supply armies. Nonetheless, Joachite patterns of thought were to be pro-

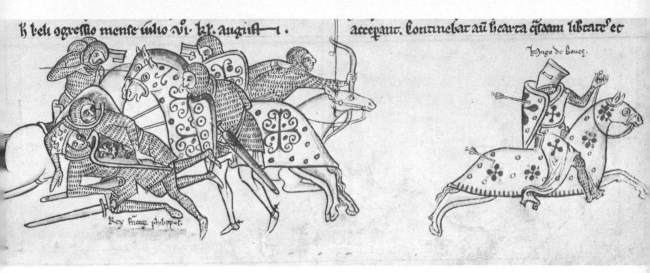

k̄ belt ogreſſio menſe iulio vi· kl· auguſt ꝉ·   accepaur. Conunebar au̅ heaṟta q̄ſdam libeṟate'er

Bey franc̄ philippuſ.

Hugo de Bouez.

foundly influential. For centuries the lunatic fringe among European intellectuals was to find the peculiar logic of Joachim's vision irresistibly attractive. Indeed it has been suggested that the phrase 'the Third Reich' would not have had the emotional appeal it did have in Germany in the 1930s were it not for the fact that Joachim's notion of a Third Age, enduring until the Last Judgment, had long ago sunk deep into the subconscious mind.

By February 1191 the army in Sicily was becoming impatient. Only Richard's generosity in distributing gifts to all and sundry held the troops together. But the enforced idleness was getting on Richard's nerves too. In this restless atmosphere it was easy for a trivial incident to be blown up out of all proportion. One day when Richard was out riding with a party of English and French knights, they met a peasant with a supply of canes. At once they took the canes and arranged an impromptu tournament. Richard clashed with William de Barres, one of the bravest of the French knights and William wielded his cane to such effect that he succeeded in damaging the King's helmet. Enraged, Richard attacked William furiously but then his saddle slipped and Richard found himself on the ground. Richard called for a fresh horse and once again tried to unseat William, but the latter clung fast to his horse's neck and could not be moved. Finding himself unable to win, Richard completely lost

The incident in the Battle of Bouvines, 1214, when Philip Augustus was unhorsed but saved by the French knight, William de Barres. Illustration from Matthew Paris's Chronica Majora.

89

his temper and ordered William never to show his face in his presence again; from now on he would look upon him as his enemy. Richard indeed forced Philip to send William away and not until the eve of the French King's departure from Sicily did Richard relent and allow William to return to his lord's service. Even then Richard gave way only after Philip and all the leading French magnates had gone down on their knees before him. More than twenty years later, in 1214, at a crucial moment in the Battle of Bouvines, William de Barres saved King Philip's life. Had the French King been killed in this battle – the climax of the struggle between England and France – King John's reputation would have been made. But, in the end, it was Philip who won the Battle of Bouvines and, as a result, a group of English barons were able to force their discredited King to seal Magna Carta.

Meanwhile, however, Richard and Philip were at odds over a matter far more serious than the consequences of William de Barres' skill with a cane. This was the question of Richard's marriage. He had been betrothed to Philip's sister, Alice, ever since 1169, but except in order to embarrass his father, he had never given any indication that he might actually go through with the marriage. Now Eleanor of Aquitaine was on her way to Sicily, bringing with her an alternative bride for Richard. This was Berengaria, daughter of the King of Navarre. Richard's mother calculated that this marriage alliance would ensure peace on the southern border of Aquitaine. Philip could hardly stand by and see his sister discarded in this insulting fashion. On the other hand, if Richard refused point blank to marry Alice, it was hard to see what he could do about it. Richard not only refused, he also told Philip that Alice had been one of Henry II's mistresses and had borne him a child. Richard claimed to have witnesses who were ready to prove this. In this difficult situation, Philip began to intrigue with Tancred, suggesting that they might unite against the over-bearing and unreliable English King. Tancred, however, calculated that Richard was a more powerful ally than Philip. At a meeting in Catania early in March, he made a treaty of friendship with him. The alliance was sealed with an exchange of gifts. Richard's present to Tancred was Excalibur, the sword which had once been owned by King Arthur. (It was at about this time that, back in England,

the tomb of Arthur and Guinevere was 'discovered' at Glaston-
bury.) After these courtesies Tancred revealed Philip's plans to
Richard and showed him the letters which the King of France
had written. Philip had over-reached himself and was now
forced to back down. In return for ten thousand marks Philip
released Richard from all promises he had made to marry Alice.
Not unnaturally, however, Philip had no wish to see the Princess who was going to supplant his sister, so, on 30 March 1191,
just a few hours before Eleanor and Berengaria arrived, his fleet
moved out of the harbour of Messina and set sail for Acre.

Eleanor stayed about three days in Messina. Then this in-
domitable old lady, now about seventy years old, set off on the
long journey back to Normandy, pausing only in Rome to
settle some of Richard's business with the Pope. We know
almost nothing about the girl whom Eleanor left behind her
in the care of Richard's sister Joan. Berengaria moves silently in
the background of events. Contemporary writers found little
in her either to praise or to blame. They dismiss her in a phrase:
'a lady of beauty and good sense' says one; 'sensible rather than
attractive' says another. In Richard's army there was a story
that Richard had long ago seen her at a tournament and had
fallen in love with her then, but this is almost certainly nothing
more than romantic gossip. After they were married, Berengaria and Richard did not spend much time together. There
were times when force of circumstances gave them no choice
in the matter, but there were times also when it is clear that
Richard preferred to do without her. For the moment, however, the wedding had to be postponed. It was Lent. Still,
though Richard could not marry in Lent, he could at least travel.
Now that Berengaria had arrived, there was no reason why he
should delay any longer in Sicily. He could marry her in the
Holy Land.

So he prepared to go. His castle of Mategriffon was dismantled and stowed away, in sections, aboard ship. Then, on
10 April 1191, Richard's huge fleet – an eye-witness counted
two hundred vessels – left Sicily behind.

*'A lady of beauty
and good sense'*

4

The Siege of Acre
1191

Richard was able to hold the greater part of the fleet together; a light was kept burning at the masthead of the King's ship as a guide to the others. But among the vessels which failed to keep in contact was the great ship carrying Berengaria and Joan. Having just dropped one fiancée it would be a pity to lose another so quickly. So when Richard reached Rhodes on 19 April he decided to stay there while he sent out fast galleys in search of the lost ship.

It was eventually found at anchor outside Limassol on the south coast of Cyprus. In company with two more ships it had been swept eastwards, and it had been most fortunate to escape the fate of the other ships which were both driven aground and wrecked. Some of the crew and passengers were drowned, including Roger Malcael, the King's Vice-Chancellor and seal-bearer. But when his body was washed ashore, the seal, which the Vice-Chancellor always wore on a chain around his neck, was recovered. Those who reached dry land were seized,

PREVIOUS PAGES The art of siege: a Muslim town being attacked by Crusaders. The garrison defends itself by shooting arrows and throwing missiles, while the attackers use catapults to break down the walls. In the centre, a tower crumbles under the assault.

RIGHT A shipwreck from the thirteenth-century chronicle of the life of Alfonso X of Castile.

stripped of all they had with them and imprisoned. A few lucky ones were able to fight their way out of captivity and join up with a landing party sent ashore from the third ship. All of them then returned to the safety of this ship where they waited to see what action the ruler of Cyprus would decide to take.

Cyprus, an island famous for its cedars and vineyards, had long been part of the Byzantine Empire, but five years previously Isaac Ducas Comnenus, a member of the imperial family, had arrived there claiming, on the basis of forged documents, to be the island's new governor, just sent out from Constantinople. His deception was successful. The island's fortresses were placed in his hands. Then Isaac threw off the mask and governed Cyprus as an independent ruler calling himself Emperor. In order to maintain himself against the government of Constantinople, Isaac had made an alliance with Saladin and, in consequence, he had no intention of giving any help to Crusaders. Ambroise, of course, was shocked by the treaty between Isaac and Saladin:

> And it was told of them as fact
> That they had sealed their friendship's pact
> By drinking one another's blood.

Crusader's bowl, decorated with the figure of a legendary griffon, from Cyprus.

95

As soon as Isaac learned of the identity of the passengers on the third ship he invited them ashore, but Joan, fearing a trap, declined the offer. Instead she asked if they might send ashore for fresh water. Isaac, however, refused this request and, in order to oppose any attempt to land in force he began to muster troops on the beach outside Limassol. All this was reported to Richard by the captain who had found the lost ship. At once Richard and his war galleys set sail for Limassol, where they arrived on 6 May. When Isaac refused to release his prisoners and restore the property which he had seized, Richard gave the order for attack. Isaac had stripped Limassol bare of everything that could be moved and could be used to fortify the beach: doors, benches, chests, planks, blocks of stone. The abandoned hulks of old ships were also pressed into service. Undaunted by the arrangements made to receive them, Richard and his men piled into small boats and rowed for the shore. As soon as they were in range, the English archers opened fire on the defenders and then, with Richard at their head, they jumped out of the boats and charged up the beach. After a brief fight the Cypriots retreated and the English marched into Limassol where they found a very satisfying amount of wine, meat and corn. That night Isaac pitched camp about five miles from the town, intending to give battle next day. But he badly under-estimated his opponent. He had been an oppressive and unpopular ruler so there were plenty of people willing to keep Richard's scouts informed of Isaac's movements and plans. While Isaac and his men slept, their camp was surrounded. As the sun rose the English troops swept through the Cypriot tents. Isaac just managed to escape, but had no time to dress first. He left behind his treasure, his horses, his arms and his imperial standard, embroidered in cloth of gold. This standard Richard afterwards presented to the abbey of Bury St Edmunds.

Isaac realised that it was useless to fight on and sent envoys to make terms with Richard. He then came himself to Richard's camp to confirm the agreement they had made. The terms were so stiff that it is unlikely that Isaac ever had any intention of keeping them – indeed it may be that he came to the camp only in order to spy on Richard's forces and obtain some idea of Richard's plans. Certainly once he had left the camp – according to one account he slipped away while Richard's men were

OPPOSITE Kantara Castle, one of the great fortresses built in the mountains of northern Cyprus.

96

Applicat Lodowicus.

Troops landing: an
illustration from Matthew
Paris's *Chronica Majora*.

having a siesta – he publicly announced that he did not consider himself bound by the terms of the agreement. It is said that
this news pleased Richard – presumably because it gave him
the justification he needed for his next great enterprise: the
conquest of Cyprus.

On 11 May, the day on which Isaac came to Richard's camp,
the English King had received other visitors. From the Holy
Land there had come Guy of Lusignan, King of Jerusalem, and
his brother Geoffrey, Bohemund, Prince of Antioch, Raymond, Count of Tripoli, Humphrey of Toron and many other
nobles and knights. They had come to ask for Richard's support
against the political manœuvres of King Philip – who had
arrived in Acre on 20 April – manœuvres which were designed
to push Guy off the throne of Jerusalem and replace him with
Conrad of Montferrat. Richard agreed; it was only natural that
he and Philip should take opposing sides. In return Guy and his
companions were to help Richard conquer Cyprus. But first
there was a marriage to be celebrated.

On 12 May Richard and Berengaria were married in the chapel
of St George at Limassol and then Berengaria was crowned
Queen by John, Bishop of Evreux. So in a Cypriot town a
Queen of England was crowned by the bishop of a Norman see.
Richard was a King of England but he was also much more
than that, and those whose lives became bound up with his

found that they had to range widely through the whole of Christendom.

The wedding over, Richard turned to the business of war. Part of his army he handed over to Guy of Lusignan, with instructions to pursue and, if possible, capture Isaac. The rest were embarked in the galleys, half of which, under his command, sailed one way round the island, while the other half, commanded by Robert of Turnham, sailed round in the opposite direction. As they circumnavigated the island they captured coastal towns and castles as well as enemy ships. Having completed their circuit they returned to Limassol where they were rejoined by Guy of Lusignan. He had not succeeded in tracking down Isaac; nevertheless, like the other commanders, he was able to report that Cypriots everywhere were prepared to recognise Richard as their lord in preference to the tyrannical self-styled emperor. Typical of the stories circulating about Isaac was one which told how he cut the nose off a noble who was honest enough to advise him to submit.

Isaac, however, was confident that he and his followers could hold out in the great fortresses perched high in the mountains of northern Cyprus: Buffavento, Kantara, Kyrenia and St Hilarion (or *Dieu d'Amour* as the Franks called it, claiming that it was the Castle of Love built for Cupid by Venus, Queen of Cyprus, a legend appropriate to the castle's romantic site). Isaac calculated that eventually Richard would have to move on to the Holy Land. When he was gone Isaac could come

A sea-battle from Matthew Paris's *Chronica Majora*. One boat has grappled another, while the combatants prepare to hurl a catapult pot of 'Greek Fire', a naptha-based mixture which burst into flame when the pots shattered.

LEFT Gilt crucifix.
BELOW Crusaders'
reliquaries contained
in crystal cases.

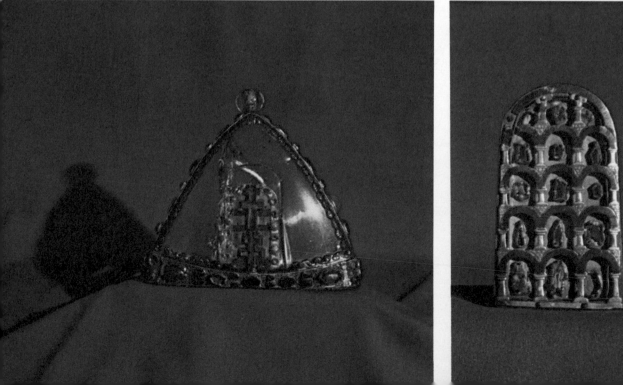

out of hiding and take over the island once again. It was not a badly-laid plan, but it came to nothing when Guy of Lusignan captured the stronghold of Kyrenia. Here Isaac had placed his wife and little daughter for, as he thought, safe-keeping. When he heard the news of their capture he was beside himself with grief and agreed to surrender, making only one condition – that he should not be put in irons. Richard therefore had silver chains made especially for him. By 1 June the whole of Cyprus was in Richard's hands. In area it was only about the size of East Anglia, but the mountainous terrain ought to have made conquest difficult. Richard, however, was much more than a dashing knight-adventurer; he was also a great general and at no time did he display his ability to greater effect than in those few weeks in Cyprus. The whole operation was brilliantly conceived and methodically carried out.

The conqueror reaped tremendous rewards. In addition to the spoils of war and the property confiscated from those who had dared to fight against him, Richard imposed a fifty per cent capital levy on every Cypriot. In return, he confirmed the traditional laws and customs of the island. But from now on, the laws were to be enforced by Angevin officials backed by Angevin garrisons. As an outward sign of the new order, Richard required all loyal Greeks to shave off their beards. They were obliged to look like Westerners. Two Englishmen, Richard of Camville and Robert of Turnham, were put in charge of the government of Cyprus.

The capture of Cyprus was vitally important to the Christians in Outremer. In face of the overwhelming superiority of the Muslim land-forces, Outremer owed its survival to sea-power. The towns on the Palestinian and Syrian coast were kept going by the men and supplies ferried across the Mediterranean by the fleets of Venice, Pisa and Genoa. But the supply line was dangerously long. After the capture of Cyprus things were much better. The Christians now held a safe island base which could be used both as a supply depot and as a springboard for future Crusades. Though safe from attack (not until 1571 did Cyprus fall to the Turks), it lay so close to the eastern shores of the Mediterranean that a man standing on the hills around Stavrovouni could see on the horizon the cedar-covered mountains of Lebanon. In strategical terms, the conquest of Cyprus

was a master-stroke. Centuries later, an observer of the re-occupation of Cyprus by British forces in 1878 commented: 'He who would become and remain a great power in the East must hold Cyprus in his hand.' Richard was well aware of the island's value. Two envoys sent by Philip had met him at Famagusta while he was still organising the war against Isaac. They had asked him to leave everything and sail at once to Acre where there were Saracens, not Christian Greeks, to be over-come. Richard was angered and gave them a piece of his mind. According to Ambroise:

> ... he lifted up his brows
> And words were said that are not fit
> Herein to be set down or writ.

But not everything that Richard said was unrepeatable. He pointed out to Philip's envoys that if the kingdom of Jerusalem were to survive it was essential for Cyprus to be in friendly hands, and that Isaac had been the ally of Saladin.

Only now was Richard ready to leave the island. Taking Isaac

and the ex-ruler's family with him, Richard set sail from Famagusta on 5 June. He made his first landfall near the great castle
of the Knights of St John at Margat. This castle was to be Isaac's
prison. Then Richard sailed south, reaching Tyre on 6 June.
The garrison of Tyre, however, would not give permission for
him to enter the town. In this they were acting on the instructions of King Philip and Conrad of Montferrat, the Lord of
Tyre. So Richard spent the night encamped outside the town
and next day continued on his voyage to Acre. Outside Acre
his fleet intercepted a large supply ship flying the flag of the
French King. On closer inspection, however, it proved to be a
blockade-runner, laden with supplies and reinforcements for
the garrison of Acre. (In an earlier, successful, attempt to run
the blockade, not only had Saladin's sailors shaved off their
beards and put on Frankish clothes, they had also ostenta-
tiously kept pigs on the ship's upper deck, relying on the
Christian patrols knowing that Muslims would never eat pork.)
Richard's galleys closed with the supply ship and, after a very
fierce struggle, the blockade runner was sunk. According to a
Muslim account, when the ship's captain saw that defeat was
inevitable he scuttled his ship rather than see valuable supplies
and siege equipment fall into enemy hands. A rumour prevalent
among the Franks said that this equipment included a stock of
two hundred snakes which the Muslims, with characteristically
evil cunning, had planned to release in the camp of the Christian
army. After this triumph Richard was given a joyous welcome
when he joined the army besieging Acre on 8 June:

> For bells they rang and trumpets blew
> Horns, pipes and other music too.
>
> (Ambroise)

The celebration lasted well into the night as the army danced
and sang by the light of torches and bonfires. Observing the
scene from the hills around Acre, Saladin's men gloomily noted
the vast amount of equipment which Richard had brought
with him.

To understand the problems facing Richard at Acre we have to
go back to June 1188. In that month Guy of Lusignan had been
released by Saladin on condition that he took no further part in

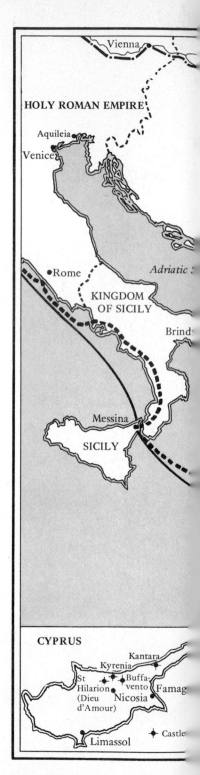

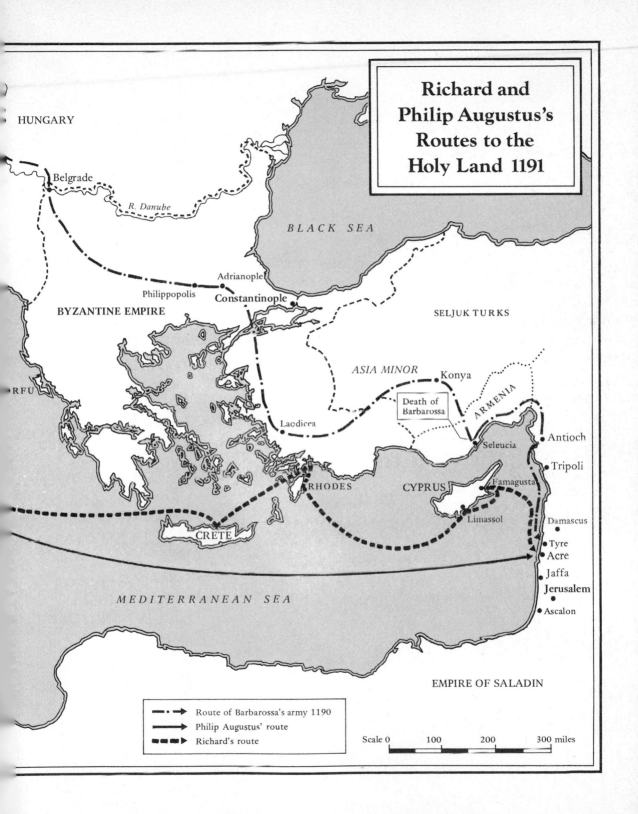

Richard and Philip Augustus's Routes to the Holy Land 1191

HUNGARY

Belgrade

R. Danube

BLACK SEA

Adrianople

Philippopolis

Constantinople

BYZANTINE EMPIRE

SELJUK TURKS

ASIA MINOR

Konya

RFU

Death of Barbarossa

ARMENIA

Laodicea

Seleucia

Antioch

Tripoli

RHODES

CYPRUS

Famagusta

CRETE

Limassol

Damascus

Tyre

Acre

Jaffa

Jerusalem

Ascalon

MEDITERRANEAN SEA

EMPIRE OF SALADIN

—·—·▶ Route of Barbarossa's army 1190

———▶ Philip Augustus' route

■■■■▶ Richard's route

Scale 0   100   200   300 miles

Nazareth
Jericho
Beethlee
vale iosaphat
IERVSALEM
templu dm
templu salomonis
Sepulchru
Arsur
ascaloine
Damiete

the fighting. Guy, of course, had no difficulty in finding a clergyman who would release him from the oath he had sworn to Saladin. Good Christians were not expected to keep the promises they made to the Infidels – 'the pagan cattle, the unbelieving black-faced brood' as Ambroise called them. Unfortunately for Guy, while he was in captivity, a new leader of the Franks had emerged. This was Conrad of Montferrat whose courageous defence of Tyre against Saladin had made him the hero of the hour. Sensing that his star was in the ascendant, Conrad had no intention of handing Tyre back to Guy, though as far as law went the town was Crown property and unquestionably belonged to the latter as King of Jerusalem. As the months went by Guy's position became more and more hopeless, then suddenly, in August 1189, he seized the initiative. He did what nobody, not Conrad, not Saladin, could possibly have imagined him doing. He marched south with a few followers and laid siege to Acre. Until its capture by Saladin in 1187,

OPPOSITE The last folio of Matthew Paris's itinerary from London to Jerusalem showing the fortresses along the Palestinian and Syrian coast, including Caesarea, Jaffa and Ascalon – and Jerusalem, with Jericho, Bethlehem, Nazareth and the Dead Sea at the top of the page.

LEFT The French King carrying out the maritime blockade and land assault on Acre in 1191.

Acre had been the chief port and the largest town in the kingdom of Jerusalem. An army the size of Guy's had no hope of taking it. When Saladin arrived on the scene Guy would be trapped between the Acre garrison and the might of the whole Muslim army. On the face of it, it was an act of incredible folly. Guy had the reputation of being a rather simple man, but nobody had thought he was as stupid as that. And yet it worked. Guy set up camp on the hill of Turon, a mile east of Acre, and although he was unable to take the city, Saladin was equally incapable of dislodging him. With each month that went by, more reinforcements streamed into the Christian camp and eventually it became possible for Guy to complete the landward blockade of Acre. The occasional supply ship got through, however, and this enabled the garrison to hold out. Thus a position of stale-mate was reached. The Christians besieged Acre and Saladin besieged the besiegers. The stale-mate was not broken until the arrival of the Kings in the spring and early summer of 1191.

Conrad of Montferrat, meanwhile, had been able to improve his legal position *vis-à-vis* Guy of Lusignan. Guy was King of Jerusalem by virtue of the fact that he had married Sibylla, the heiress to the kingdom. But during the autumn of 1190 Guy lost both his wife and their two daughters, victims of one of the epidemics which were a normal part of life in the unhealthy atmosphere of a medieval army camp. As in most wars disease did more damage than the weapons of the human enemy. With Sibylla dead, could Guy still claim to be King? Or was it Sibylla's younger sister, Isabella, who inherited her rights? It seemed to Conrad that Isabella ought to be Queen and that he was just the sort of man to be her husband. True, it was rumoured that at least one of Conrad's two previous wives – one Italian, one Greek – was still alive, but then army gossip was notoriously unreliable. It was true also that Isabella had a husband already, Humphrey of Toron; he was unquestionably alive, indeed he was there in the camp. But then there were churchmen in the camp too, and wherever there were churchmen, there marriages could be broken. If the Archbishop of Canterbury would not annul the marriage – and Baldwin, who had arrived in October 1190, did in fact refuse to do so – then Conrad could try the Archbishop of Pisa. And so it was done.

OPPOSITE Two knights jousting, from the *Luttrell Psalter* of 1340. The artist has given the knight on the left the arms of Richard I of England, while the knight on the right bears the shield of a Saracen's head and has a suitably villainous face to represent the Infidel Saladin.

confitebor illi: salutare uultus mei
t deus meus.

Ad me ipsum anima mea turba
ta est: propterea memor ero tui de
terra iordanis.t hermonium a mon
te modico.

Abyssus abissum inuocat: in uo
ce catharactarum tuarum.

Omnia excelsa tua t fluctus tui:
super me transierunt.

In die mandauit dominus miseri
cordiam suam:t nocte canticu eius.

Apud me oracio deo uite mee: di
cam deo susceptor meus es.

Humphrey, who had no desire to be king of a kingdom which still had to be fought for, and who was, in any case, notoriously effeminate, made no objection. If Isabella objected, her feelings on the matter were held to be of no account. In November she and Conrad were married by the Bishop of Beauvais, a cousin of the King of France. Now there were two candidates for the throne.

Richard, therefore, had two problems to tackle. First, of course, Acre had to be taken. But then the much more difficult question of the quarrel between Guy and Conrad would have to be faced. For the moment, however, all parties were united in their determination to capture Acre. For two years, all eyes in the Muslim as well as in the Christian world, had been focussed on this one city. If it fell it would be the first great set-back in Saladin's career and a severe blow to the prestige of the victor of Hattin. Richard's arrival stimulated the besiegers to greater efforts and put fear into the hearts of the enemy. His reputation had come before him. The wooden castle of Mategriffon was raised again, this time outside the gate of Acre.

The bombardment of the city walls was intensified as Richard brought his stone-throwing catapults up to join those erected by Philip, by the Duke of Burgundy and by the Hospitallers and Templars. Philip's best catapult was given the traditional name of 'Malvoisin', 'Bad Neighbour', while another such siege-machine, built with money from the Crusaders' common purse, was called 'God's Own Catapult'. The defenders of Acre

The Byzantine fleet destroying the enemy by the use of 'Greek Fire'. Water could not extinguish the fire, so that it could be used to great effect in sea battles.

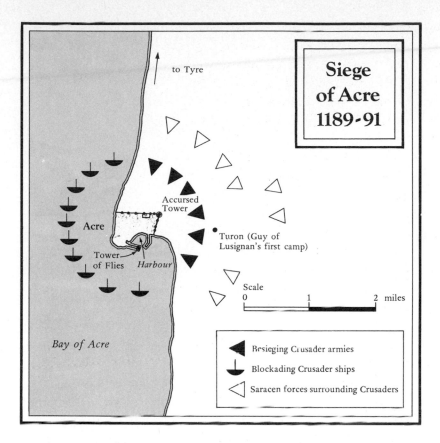

to Tyre

**Siege
of Acre
1189-91**

Accursed
Tower

Acre

Turon (Guy of
Lusignan's first camp)

Tower
of Flies   *Harbour*

Scale

0   1   2 miles

Bay of Acre

Besieging Crusader armies

Blockading Crusader ships

Saracen forces surrounding Crusaders

directed their own artillery fire against the Frankish siege-machines. Being made of wood they were particularly vulnerable to the dreaded Greek Fire. This was a naphtha-based mixture which was put into pots and then hurled from catapults. On impact the pots were shattered and the mixture burst into flames. In order to put out Greek Fire one had to have containers full of vinegar ready to hand – water was no use at all. For this reason Greek Fire could be at its most devastating in sea-battles. On several occasions King Philip's siege-machines were put out of action by well-aimed Greek Fire. Nonetheless, slowly but surely, the walls of Acre were battered down.

Every now and then, a section of wall collapsed as a result of being undermined. Undermining was the most efficient method of bringing down a wall. The miners tunnelled their way beneath the foundations which they underpinned with timber props. The mine was then filled with brushwood, logs and other combustible material. When all was ready, this was set alight

and the miners beat a hasty retreat. The props were burned through, the masonry above collapsed – and hopefully a party of assailants was ready and waiting to storm through the breach. There was only one way by which the defenders could meet the threat of a mine: they had to dig a counter-mine. That meant tunnelling into the mine from their side and then capturing it. The fate of a besieged town or castle would very often hinge upon the outcome of those desperate hand-to-hand struggles which took place in the darkness below ground. At one stage, in his anxiety to break down the wall, Richard was willing to offer gold-pieces to any man who could bring him back a stone. For the soldiers to get at the wall it was necessary to fill the moat in – with earth, rubble and all kinds of rubbish. There is a story told of one enthusiastic woman who, on being mortally wounded, begged that her body should be thrown into the moat so that even when dead she could continue to be of use to the besiegers.

Shortly after Richard's arrival, both he and Philip fell ill. The chronicles called their illness *Arnaldia* or *Leonardie*, a fever which caused their hair and nails to fall out. It was probably a form of scurvy or trench mouth. At one point Richard became so seriously ill that his life was thought to be in danger. But as soon as his condition began to improve he insisted that he should be carried to the front-line in a litter so that he could continue to direct siege-operations.

At regular intervals, when the Kings judged that the artillery bombardment had sufficiently softened up the target, they gave the order for an assault against some weak point in the city walls. When they saw the Franks advancing, the defenders of Acre beat their drums as a signal to Saladin. He immediately launched an attack against the camp of the besiegers who were thus forced to fight on two fronts. Time and again the assault was driven back. Nonetheless the sustained pressure was taking its toll. Inside Acre the beleaguered garrison was running short of food and war materials. The coming of the English and French fleets meant that Muslim supply-ships could no longer hope to get through. The garrison kept in touch with Saladin by using carrier-pigeons, and occasionally a messenger was able to swim through the Frankish lines. But after nearly two years of siege, the defenders of Acre were exhausted and they needed

OPPOSITE Page from the thirteenth-century Chronicle of Alfonso X of Castile, showing Arabs and Christians in battle. The Christians carry into battle a standard bearing the image of the Virgin with Christ.

During the siege of Acre, Richard I offered a gold piece to any man who could bring him back a stone from the walls of the city.

something more than messages of encouragement. Their courage was tremendous and compelled admiration even in the Christian camp. 'What can we say of this race of infidels who thus defended their city? Never were there braver soldiers than these, the honour of their nation. If only they had been of the true faith it would not have been possible, anywhere in the world, to find men to surpass them.' But courage alone was no longer enough. On 3 July Saladin made a last bid to take the besiegers' camp by storm. When this failed, the capitulation of Acre became both inevitable and imminent.

On 12 July besiegers and besieged agreed on terms of surrender. The lives of the defenders were to be spared in return for a ransom of two hundred thousand gold pieces (dinars), for the release of fifteen hundred prisoners now in Saladin's hands and for the restoration of the Holy Cross. When he heard of the conditions Saladin was horrified, but it was too late – the Frankish banners were already waving over the city. Acre had fallen at last.

But as the Christian army moved in to take possession of the captured city there occurred a fateful incident which was to have far-reaching consequences. Duke Leopold of Austria planted his banner by the side of the standards belonging to the Kings of France and England. For a brief while it stood there in triumph, but then some English soldiers tore it down and threw it into a ditch. Leopold was naturally offended. A few days later, having tried in vain to obtain satisfaction, he left Acre and returned to Austria. Correctly enough he held Richard responsible for the insult. The English soldiers must have acted with, at the very least, their lord's tacit approval. Leopold had good cause to hate the English King and two years later, when Richard fell into his hands, he took his revenge.

What was it that lay behind the incident of the standard? Why did Richard humiliate Leopold? Was it nothing more than a gratuitous insult? To understand what it was all about, we have to look more closely at Leopold of Austria's position in the Crusader camp. Leopold had reached Acre in spring 1191, somewhat earlier than the two Kings. From the moment of his arrival he found himself cast in the rôle of leader of the German contingent. Compared with the numbers of French and English, there were, however, very few Germans present. The great

German Crusade had broken up after the death of Frederick Barbarossa. Only a pitifully small remnant of Barbarossa's army managed to struggle on as far as Acre. They arrived there in October 1190, carrying with them some bones from the body of the dead Emperor – bones which they hoped would one day find a fitting resting place in Jerusalem. In command of this contingent was Barbarossa's son, Duke Frederick of Swabia. In January 1191, however, Frederick's name was added to the long list of those who had succumbed to the diseases of the camp. Thus when Leopold of Austria arrived at Acre in the spring of 1191 he found himself the most important German noble present. But despite his splendid connections – he was related to both the Hohenstaufen and the Comneni – Leopold did not have the resources to make his presence felt in the Frankish camp. His own retinue was tiny and he did not have the cash to attract other men to his banner. (King Philip, on arriving at Acre, had offered three gold pieces a month to all who would serve under him, only to be outbid by Richard who, typically, had offered four.) Indeed, according to one English chronicler, Leopold was able to stay in Outremer only because he was subsidised by the wealthy King of England. Leopold remained an unimportant outsider in a camp which had split into two factions. For him to raise his standard in Acre was totally unrealistic.

What we have to remember is that when an army commander planted his banner in a captured town, he was not merely announcing his triumph to the world, he was also staking his claim to the loot. Thus if the two Kings had allowed Leopold's standard to remain there they would, in effect, have publicly acknowledged that the Duke of Austria was entitled to share the plunder with them. Yet, as we know, right from the start of the Crusade, Richard and Philip had acted on the assumption that they would each take one half. Only recently indeed, while they were both lying sick outside the walls of Acre, the two Kings – who were never too sick to quarrel – had again quarrelled over booty. Philip had demanded a half of Cyprus and Richard had countered by requiring Philip to hand over half of Artois. For Count Philip of Flanders had died at Acre on 1 June and by the terms of a treaty which he had made with Philip of France in 1186, this death meant that the French

King was the new Lord of Artois. Though neither King gave in to the demands of the other, the argument shows that they were still thinking in terms of a fifty-fifty division of the spoils. If Richard was not prepared to change the arrangement now, this was not because he was a niggardly, avaricious man. On the contrary, he was a generous lord who rewarded in magnificent fashion the men who served him. But Leopold of Austria did not serve him, and if Richard was to be as generous as his own men expected him to be, then he could not afford to see a large part of the plunder slip out of his control. Duke Leopold was certainly not the only one to resent the way in which the newly arrived Kings monopolised the rewards. There were many barons and knights who, having endured the rigours of the siege for months or even years, now found themselves out in the cold. Robbed of their just reward they were too poor to do anything but return home. Naturally they complained bitterly of the greed of the English and French and, in a sense, Leopold had been acting as their spokesman. Undoubtedly, throughout the whole of this affair, Philip had taken the same line as Richard, but it was Richard who acted - and acted in a characteristically direct and high-handed fashion.

Acre had fallen. It was a great triumph, but in the moment of victory the seeds of trouble had been sown.

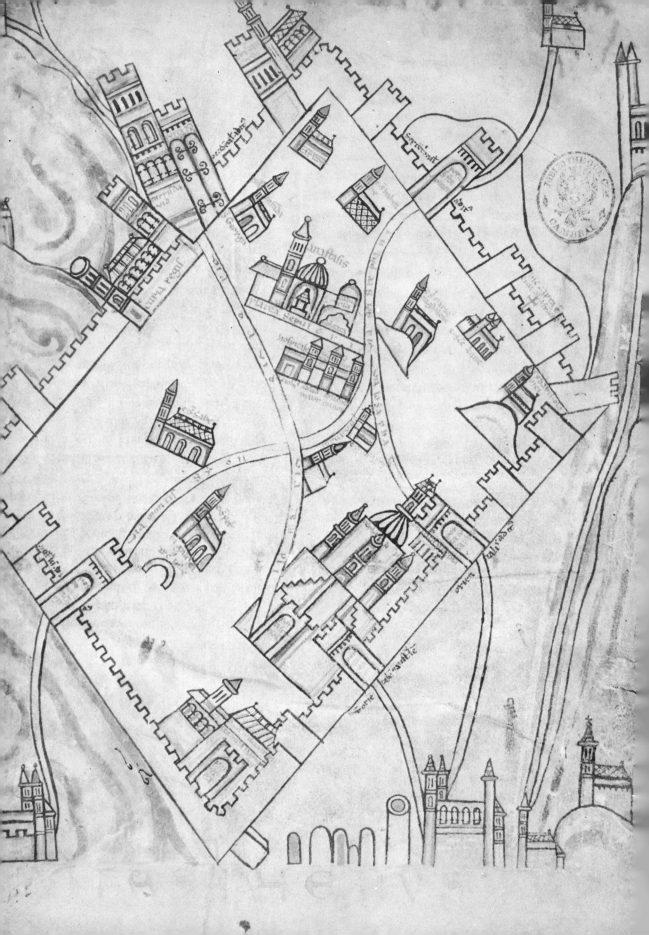

5
The Road to Jerusalem
1191-2

WITH ACRE ONCE AGAIN a Christian city, the first task of the Crusaders was to re-consecrate the churches. Their religious duty done, the Crusaders turned to politics, to the thorny question of the crown of Jerusalem. Who had the right to wear it, Guy of Lusignan or Conrad of Montferrat? After some discussion, a compromise solution was found. Richard's candidate, Guy, was to remain King till his death, then the crown should pass to Conrad and Isabella and their descendants. Meanwhile Guy and Conrad were to share the royal revenues.

Now King Philip declared his intention of going home. He had never wanted to be a Crusader; he had been ill, and an army camp in the Middle East was a hypochondriac's nightmare. Moreover, he had a very good reason for wanting to be back in France as soon as possible. His share of the inheritance of Philip of Flanders meant more to him than the fame acquired by a successful Crusader. If he wanted to make sure of Artois then to Artois he must go. In vain Richard pressed Philip to join him in a declaration of their intention to stay three years in the Holy Land. In vain the leading men in the French army, tears in their eyes, begged their lord to stay. On 31 July the King of France left Acre. He was accompanied as far as Tyre by Conrad of Montferrat to whom he had given his share of the plunder of Acre, including half the prisoners. Conrad had no wish to remain in a camp dominated by the patron of Guy of Lusignan.

PREVIOUS PAGES Detail from a twelfth-century map of Crusader Jerusalem.

BELOW Philip Augustus leaving Palestine, from the fourteenth-century *Chroniques de St Denis*.

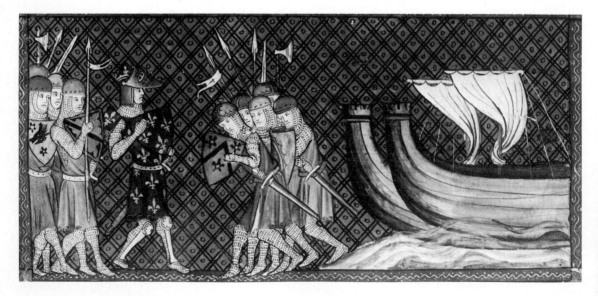

On 3 August Philip embarked at Tyre and sailed for home. With him went Roger of Howden. But the historian now has new sources to fill the gap left by the departure of this excellent guide. There is the chronicle written by Ernoul, squire to Balian of Ibelin, one of the leading barons of Outremer. Balian supported Conrad of Montferrat, and so Ernoul's work is sympathetic towards Philip and frankly hostile to Richard. Richard's admirers, of course, returned the compliment. Ambroise wrote:

> There was Balian of Ibelin
> Falser than any friend of sin.

But above all, there are now the accounts written by Arab historians, particularly Baha ad-Din and Imad ad-Din, both of whom were members of Saladin's household, and very close to the master they loved. It is interesting to read the comparisons they made between the Kings of England and France. Baha ad-Din wrote that Richard was 'a man of great courage and spirit. He had fought great battles and showed a burning passion for war. His kingdom and standing were inferior to those of the French king, but his wealth, reputation and valour were greater.' Presumably Richard's royal dignity seemed to be less than Philip's, because the Muslims knew that Richard did homage to Philip for his Continental possessions, but it is clear that they feared the English King more. Elsewhere Baha ad-Din refers to the 'cunning of this accursed man [i.e. Richard]. To gain his ends he uses now soft words, now violent deeds. God alone was able to save us from his malice. Never have we had to face a subtler or a bolder opponent.'

The English, of course, looked upon Philip's departure as traitorous desertion and they wondered what he would do once he was back in France. Richard had his suspicions. He obtained from Philip a promise that he would not attack Richard's territories while Richard was away on Crusade. But like most kings Philip found it hard to keep his promises. Friends of the French King have pointed out that a large part of his army stayed behind in the Holy Land under the command of the Duke of Burgundy. Unfortunately, although Philip also left some of his treasure, the Duke did not have the financial resources to maintain an army of this size for long. So Richard had to step in and advance the money. Yet Richard must have felt that

Philip's going was not all loss. In the expressive phrase of the Winchester chronicler, Richard of Devizes, Philip was to Richard like a hammer tied to the tail of a cat. Now, at least, there could be no doubt about who was in supreme command. It was, for example, up to Richard alone to see that Saladin implemented the terms of the treaty made by his officers at Acre.

This was not going to be easy. The first step was to secure the return of the Muslim prisoners who had been moved to Tyre. Conrad was obstinate, however, and only when the Duke of Burgundy went to Tyre in person did he agree to hand them back. Apart from this Conrad would do nothing to help Richard, even though Richard was fighting to win a kingdom which Conrad could expect to inherit. Saladin also had his problems. The terms of the Acre treaty had deeply shocked him; possibly he simply did not have an organisation capable of bringing together so much money and so many prisoners by the stipulated date – a month after the fall of Acre. The details of the negotiations about the implementation of the treaty are obscure. The Christian and the Muslim versions differ considerably, but it seems that Richard was willing to allow Saladin to pay in instalments and that he himself was prepared to release the prisoners as soon as the first instalment had been received. Unfortunately on the day the first instalment was due Saladin was still not quite ready. He offered to hand over the men and money that he had and to give hostages as a guarantee that the transfer would be completed; in return he wanted Richard either to free the prisoners at once or to give hostages as a guarantee that he would free them. Richard, however, insisted that Saladin hand over the bulk of the men and money at once and be satisfied with his royal promise that the prisoners would be released when the instalment had been paid in full. This Saladin was not prepared to do. Richard therefore argued that the lives of the Acre garrison were forfeit and set 20 August as the date of execution. Saladin still would not accept Richard's terms; indeed in the Frankish camp there was a rumour – almost certainly false – that he had killed his own prisoners. So, on 20 August, on Richard's orders, two thousand seven hundred members of the Acre garrison were taken outside the city walls and there, in full view of Saladin's helpless army,

they were massacred. According to Ambroise, the Christian soldiers delighted in the work of butchery, seeing it as revenge for the deaths of their fellows who had been killed during the siege. Another chronicler says that the bodies were disembowelled and that a great quantity of gold and silver was found in the entrails. Only the most important members of the garrison were spared; they might fetch large ransoms or come in useful later should an exchange of distinguished prisoners be desired.

Of all Richard's deeds, this is the one most bitterly criticised. It has been called both barbarous and stupid. But in the eyes of a Christian king of the twelfth century, the lives of the unbelievers were of no account. They were, in any case, doomed to hell. There was even some virtue in accelerating the process. 'The Christian glories in the death of a pagan,' said St Bernard of Clairvaux, 'because thereby Christ himself is glorified.' If the lives of the Acre garrison had any value, it was as bargaining counters. So Richard had deprived himself of a bargaining counter and the money which had been collected for the ransom Saladin now distributed among his troops. But Richard wanted to move on; he was not interested in a bargaining

Richard I watching the beheading of the Muslim garrison of Acre on 20 August 1191. Illustration from the fifteenth-century *Livres des passages d'Outremer*.

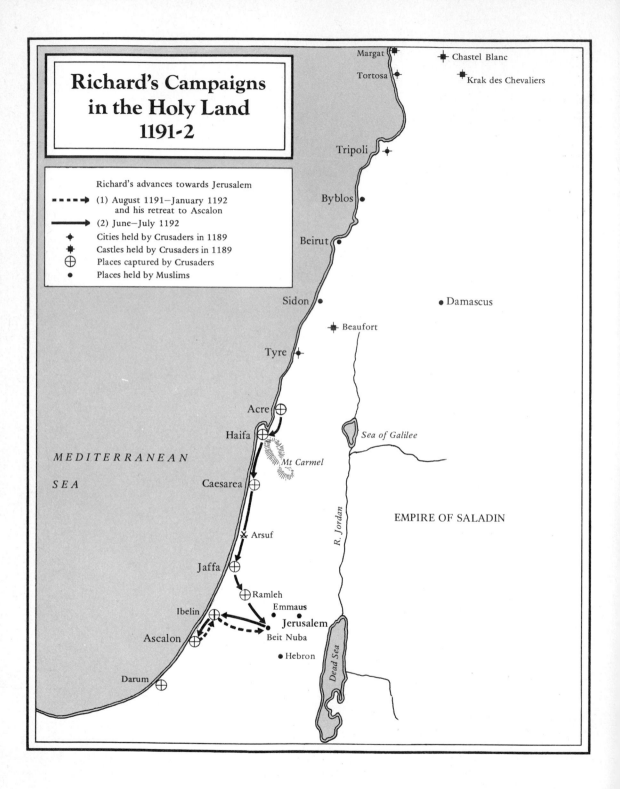

Richard's Campaigns in the Holy Land 1191-2

Richard's advances towards Jerusalem

- - - ▶ (1) August 1191–January 1192
    and his retreat to Ascalon
——▶ (2) June–July 1192
✦ Cities held by Crusaders in 1189
✚ Castles held by Crusaders in 1189
⊕ Places captured by Crusaders
• Places held by Muslims

Margat

Chastel Blanc

Tortosa

Krak des Chevaliers

Tripoli

Byblos

Beirut

Sidon

Damascus

Beaufort

Tyre

MEDITERRANEAN

SEA

Acre

Haifa

Sea of Galilee

Mt Carmel

Caesarea

Arsuf

R. Jordan

EMPIRE OF SALADIN

Jaffa

Ramleh

Emmaus

Ibelin

Jerusalem

Ascalon

Beit Nuba

Hebron

Darum

Dead Sea

counter which tied him to Acre while Saladin spun out the negotiations. And could he afford to march away leaving only a garrison to guard nearly three thousand Turks? Merely to feed so many men would be difficult enough since, on Saladin's orders, the countryside around Acre had been thoroughly devastated. The prisoners, in fact, had become an embarrassment rather than an asset and Richard had no compunction in ridding himself of them in a fashion that was brutally efficient.

Two days later Richard led the army out of Acre. It had not been easy to persuade the soldiers to leave. Acre had been a safe haven of pleasure. Saladin's secretary, the historian Imad ad-Din, described in splendidly baroque language the activities of the prostitutes who had flocked to do business with Crusaders:

> Tinted and painted, desirable and appetizing – bold and ardent, with nasal voices and fleshy thighs, ... they offered their wares for enjoyment, brought their silver anklets up to touch their golden ear-rings, ... made themselves targets for men's darts, offered themselves to the lance's blows, made javelins rise towards shields. ... They interwove leg with leg, caught lizard after lizard in their holes, guided pens to inkwells, torrents to the valley bottom, swords to scabbards, firewood to stoves ... and they maintained that this was an act of piety without equal, especially to those who were far from home and wives.

These ladies, however, had to stay behind in Acre. Washerwomen were still the only camp-followers whom Richard would allow to accompany the army on its march.

The goal of the march was Jerusalem, but it would have been foolhardy in the extreme to attempt to go there directly from Acre. The land was hilly and the supply line from the coast would have been impossibly long. So Richard decided to make for Jaffa. From there he would strike inland to Jerusalem. Whatever route he chose, he was now going to face the Turkish cavalry – the élite troops of Saladin's army – in open country. At Acre the besiegers had been safely entrenched behind their own line of fortifications and the renowned Turkish cavalry had never had a real opportunity to demonstrate their skill. At Acre the Franks faced military problems no different from those they would have faced in any siege of a similar town in Europe. But now Richard would have to cope with an unfamiliar style of warfare. He was to pass the test with flying

OVERLEAF Saladin's army, from the *Roman de Godefrey de Bouillon*.

colours because he knew how to make the best use of local advice and local experience.

The very different cavalry tactics employed by the Turks and the Franks make a fascinating contrast. The Turks were essentially mounted archers, though they each carried a small round shield and a lance, sword or club as well as their bow. All their weapons, however, were lighter than those used by the Franks and in a hand-to-hand fight between equal numbers, the Franks held the advantage. The Turks therefore used the speed and agility of their horses to stay at a distance while sending in a rain of arrows upon their enemies. They used the bow while riding at speed with such dexterity that even in retreat they could turn in the saddle and shoot at their pursuers. They used their mobility to encircle the enemy and assail him from all sides at once. Only when their archery had reduced the enemy to a state of near helplessness did the Turks shoulder their bows and ride in for the kill.

The chief tactical weapon of the Franks was the charge of their heavily armoured knights. Holding reins and shield in his left hand, the knight held a lance rigid beneath his right arm, using the forward momentum of his horse to give power to the blow delivered by the lance. If his lance shattered on impact the knight carried on the fight with his sword. The weight of the charge was such that no body of troops could stand up to it. It was said that a Frank on horseback could make a hole through the walls of Babylon. If the Franks succeeded in delivering a charge against the main body of the enemy, they won the battle. It was as simple as that – or as difficult. If the timing of the charge were fractionally wrong, the elusive Turkish cavalry was able to scatter, leaving the Franks beating against thin air. And once the charge had been delivered, the Franks, having lost their tight formation, became vulnerable to counter-attack. The Turkish horse-archers swarmed all around their enemy like gnats round a man's head. To try to drive them away with a charge was all too often like using one's hands to beat off the gnats. The only observable result was a temporary agitation in the swarm. The Turks would turn again and harrass the ponderous knights to their doom. Thus the charge had to be held back until exactly the right moment – and dashing knights did

The Frankish army, as depicted in the *Roman de Girard de Roussillon*, an early thirteenth-century French manuscript.
LEFT The great strength of the Frankish armies was the charge of the heavily-armed knights.
BELOW A knight charging with his lance, while protected by his shield.

not always find it easy to be patient when under non-stop fire. Except at close range, the light Turkish bow did not have the power to fire an arrow capable of piercing a coat of mail and wounding the body of the wearer, but it could penetrate far enough to stick in the mail, so that knights under Turkish attack were often thought to resemble porcupines. More serious than his undignified appearance was the fact that the knight was liable to have his horse killed under him. It was in this situation that the footsoldier came into his own. The knights and their horses had to be protected until the moment to charge came. The job of protecting them was given to the infantry, both spearmen and archers. They were drawn up in a defensive screen, surrounding the knights like a wall.

Richard's march south to Jaffa was a classic demonstration of Frankish military tactics at their best. He marched close to the seashore. Thus the army's right flank was protected by the sea and Richard's fleet; the speed of the advance was dictated by the speed of the ships which often had to contend with contrary winds. The knights were organised in three divisions with their left flank protected by infantry. Since this meant that the foot soldiers had to bear the brunt of the ceaseless Turkish attack, Richard divided them into two alternating halves; one half marched on the left, while the other took things easy, marching beside the baggage train between the knights and the sea.

Saladin, too, marched south, on a parallel course, keeping the main body of his troops at some distance from the Franks and sending in bands of skirmishers to harrass them continually. Richard's men were under orders to ignore all provocations and to keep marching in close formation. No one was to break ranks. Saladin naturally concentrated on the rearguard where Richard's infantry had the awkward job of facing about and fighting off the Turkish attacks while marching backwards. On the very first day of the march the rearguard – the French troops under the Duke of Burgundy – lagged behind and took a severe hammering. Richard himself rushed back from the van and saved the situation. But it was a useful lesson. From then on Richard's orders were rigidly obeyed. Ambroise noted that the soldiers marched in such tight order that it was impossible to throw an apple into the ranks without it hitting a man or a horse. One other happy result of that first day was the healing

LEFT A sword of the
Crusader period, *c.* 1250.
BELOW Thirteenth-
century battle axe of the
type used by Crusader
knights.

of an old enmity. The French knight William de Barres fought
so gallantly that Richard decided to forget the grudge he had
borne for so long.

Day after day the army toiled on, past Haifa, over the ridge
of Mount Carmel, and on past Caesarea. Everywhere they
found that Saladin's men had been there before them, razing
fortresses to the ground and burning the crops. But the presence
of the fleet enabled Richard to keep his men supplied. The heat
was intense, and the Franks, heavily armoured, suffered badly.
Sunstroke claimed many victims. And every day the arrows
of the Turks claimed many more. Richard himself was wounded
in the side, not very seriously. Yet still the army, in close formation, moved doggedly on. It was not to be harrassed into defeat.
By early September, Saladin had realised that his only hope of
stopping it lay in committing his own forces to a full-scale
pitched battle. He picked as his battle-ground the plain to the
north of Arsuf. A forest, lying to the east of the route the Crusaders had to take, would shelter the main Turkish army until
it was ready to attack. On 5 September, under a flag of truce,
Richard asked for a parley. Saladin sent his brother al-Adil to
meet him. Since Richard simply demanded the cession of the
whole of Palestine, the negotiations produced no result.
Clearly Richard cannot have expected his demands to be taken
seriously; but by talking to al-Adil he hoped to gain some
insight into Saladin's plans. On 7 October Richard once again
gave the order for the advance. In the van he placed the Templars; next came the Bretons and the men of Anjou, then King
Guy with the Poitevins; in the fourth division marched the
Normans and the English, guarding the royal standard; after
them came the French contingents, and bringing up the rear, in
the position of greatest danger, the Hospitallers. As always the

infantry had their vital defensive rôle to play. The only difference between the Battle of Arsuf and the fighting of the last two and a half weeks was that, by committing his main force to the attack, Saladin would be giving Richard a chance to deliver one of the famous Frankish charges, and if Richard could seize the moment, victory would be his.

The action began in the middle of the morning. Shouting fiercely and accompanied by beating drums and clashing cymbals, Saladin's men moved forward. Although the spears and arrows of the Christian infantry took heavy toll, the Turkish forces, supported by Bedouin and Nubian auxiliaries, seemed to be everywhere, their horsemen charging in, then wheeling round and charging again, pressing closer and closer. The rain of arrows was so thick that it obscured the light of the sun or so it seemed to Ambroise:

> Well can I recount
> That neither rain nor snow nor sleet
> In winter's depth did ever beat
> More thickly or more densely fly
> (Many can tell ye if I lie)
> Than did the foemen's shafts, which flew
> Upon us and our horses slew.

In the rearguard the Hospitallers came under terrible pressure. Several times during the day, the Master of the Hospital begged for permission to charge. Each time Richard said no; they must wait until he gave the signal for a general assault and that would not be until the entire Turkish army was closely engaged and their horses had begun to tire. The Hospitallers held on grimly. As the day wore on, the heat became more and more oppressive. The Hospitallers began to feel that the signal would never come and that they would be branded as cowards for submitting so meekly to the Turkish onslaught. Moreover they were losing horses at an alarming rate. Goaded beyond endurance, two of the knights, the Marshal of the Order and Baldwin of Carew, lost their nerve and charged. At once the rest of the Hospitallers galloped after them, scattering the infantry screen which was unprepared for this sudden move. Richard had no choice but to follow their lead. He gave the order to charge and, in order to be in a position to restore some semblance of order, he rode at the head of the knights. The massed Frankish cavalry swept all before it.

> Their soldiers stood aghast
> For we descended on the foes
> Like thunder, and great dust arose.
> Then ye had seen bearded Turks lie slain
> As thick and close as sheaves of grain.
>
> (Ambroise)

The Turks fled, but under a shrewd captain like Saladin it was at precisely this moment that they were most dangerous. If in their excitement the Franks pressed the charge too far, the knights, having lost their close order, could find that they had galloped headlong into a trap. Richard, of course, was alive to the danger. He took control, halted the charge and re-formed his line. Thus when the Turks rallied he was able to meet them with a disciplined and effective charge. The day was won. The army continued with its southward march.

Saladin's prestige had suffered a second great blow. First Acre, now Arsuf. The legend of his invincibility had been destroyed. His troops were demoralised and unwilling to face the Franks again in pitched battle. By contrast Richard now stood at the height of his fame. Although the Hospitallers had anticipated his signal they had done so by only a few minutes and Richard's quick response and masterful handling of the situation in the next crucial moments had ensured victory. Naturally his soldiers praised – and doubtless magnified – Richard's own part in the hand-to-hand combat. 'There the King, the fierce, the extraordinary King, cut down the Turks in every direction, and none could escape the force of his arm, for wherever he turned, brandishing his sword, he carved a wide path for himself, cutting them down like a reaper with his sickle.' Richard's bravery and prowess inspired the loyalty and admiration of his followers, but it was his superb generalship which really counted.

Three days later, on 10 September, the Frankish army reached Jaffa. In destroying its walls, Saladin had done so much damage that the army could find no lodging within the town; so they camped in an olive grove outside. Richard now held the port nearest Jerusalem. The obvious course was to march inland and

'None could escape the force of his arm'

head directly for the Holy City. But did Richard have enough troops to lay siege to Jerusalem and protect his supply line? If Saladin succeeded in cutting his communications, Richard would be in serious trouble. In his march from Acre to Jaffa, Richard had relied heavily on his fleet; inland the Turkish harrassing tactics might be far more effective. The main Turkish army moreover, although it had been defeated, was still intact. It lurked at Ramleh, while Saladin himself took a contingent to Ascalon further down the coast. The great harbour fortress of

One of Richard's favourite pastimes, when he was not engaged in fighting, was hawking, and birds of prey were a precious commodity in the twelfth century. This ivory cover shows a hawking party in the mid-fourteenth century.

Ascalon was the key to the vital road which linked Egypt and Syria. Saladin wanted to defend both Jerusalem and Ascalon, but in the opinion of his emirs he did not have enough troops and they forced him to choose between them. Saladin opted to hold Jerusalem. This meant that he had to dismantle Ascalon to prevent a useful base from falling, intact, into Christian hands. On the day on which Richard entered Jaffa, Saladin began to evacuate the population of Ascalon.

What would Richard do now? Sensing the strategic importance of Ascalon, he had no wish to let Saladin demolish the town unhindered. But the majority of the army argued in favour of staying where they were and re-fortifying Jaffa, on the grounds that it was a more convenient port for Jerusalem. Reluctantly, Richard agreed to this, particularly since the army needed a rest after its exertions on the way from Acre. The decisions made in September 1191 are a useful reminder that neither Saladin nor Richard was an autocratic ruler; both were forced to take account of the feelings of the men on whose co-operation they relied if they were to achieve anything. So the Franks settled down to rebuild Jaffa and enjoy the comforts of the town, the local fruit and the women who travelled down from Acre to entertain them:

> Back to the host the women came
> And plied the trade of lust and shame. (Ambroise)

But Jaffa was a small town and, after a while, some of the soldiers hankered after the more hectic excitements of Acre. Richard himself was forced to go to Acre and haul them back to their duty. When he returned, he brought with him Berengaria and Joan. The countryside around Jaffa was very pleasant and Richard took the opportunity to relax with a little hawking. But the enemy were never far away and on one occasion he was very nearly captured. A Turkish patrol stumbled across the King's party while he was taking a nap after a tiring morning's sport. Only the presence of mind of one of his escort who managed to trick the Turks into thinking that he was the King, enabled Richard to escape. Despite the warnings of his friends, Richard was always inclined to take this kind of risk. As a general he was cautious and calculating; he would never endanger the lives of his troops if he could possibly help it. But as

The game of chess was introduced by the Arabs, who also passed on many of their names to the moves. The words 'check' and 'mate' are derived from the Arabic '*Shah mat*', 'the King is dead'. According to tradition, the first Western Europeans to play chess were the men of the First Crusade. In fact, however, the game was introduced before this. Although chess was frequently denounced by Churchmen, it was certainly played by Richard and his followers during the Third Crusade. This illustration of knights playing chess is taken from the thirteenth-century *Roman de Girard de Roussillon*.

an individual he performed acts of incredible recklessness with complete nonchalance – and for years he got away with it.

In the meanwhile, he had once again opened negotiations with Saladin who, as usual, was represented by his brother al-Adil Saif-ed-Din, whom the Franks called Safadin. He was a diplomat of consummate skill and, after Saladin's death, it fell to him to hold the empire together. By negotiating separately with both Richard and Conrad of Montferrat, he gave the Franks good cause to fear a split in the Christian camp. Richard began by demanding Jerusalem and the whole of the area west of the Jordan. In reply, Saladin pointed out that the Muslims looked upon Jerusalem as a Holy City. For them it was the place from which Mahomet ascended to Heaven. Saladin claimed that even if he wanted to cede Jerusalem, popular indignation would force him to reconsider. (And it is true that when Jerusalem was restored to the Christians in 1229, it was immediately – if only temporarily – recaptured by a host of poorly armed Muslim peasants.)

Richard's next suggestion was a startlingly original one. Like the rest of the Crusaders he admired al-Adil. If Saladin would grant Palestine to his brother, then he, Richard, would arrange for al-Adil to marry his sister Joan. As a dowry he would give her the coastal cities from Acre to Ascalon. The happy couple could live at Jerusalem, to which the Christians should be given free access. Al-Adil was intrigued by the idea and passed it on to Saladin who accepted it at once, somewhat to the surprise of his advisers. But he explained that he knew that Richard regarded the whole thing as a joke. Sure enough, when al-Adil's envoy next saw Richard, the King told him that Joan had flown into a towering rage when she heard of her brother's plan, swearing that she would never consent to being an Infidel's wife. Perhaps, Richard slyly suggested, the best way of solving the problem would be for al-Adil to turn Christian. Later on, Richard had the idea of substituting his niece Eleanor of Brittany for the reluctant Joan. Unquestionably, these negotiations were not to be taken at face-value. Richard was not the man to be caught in a fog of romantic optimism. He was mustering an army ready to move out of Jaffa and in the meantime was becoming acquainted with the enemy. All contacts, however lighthearted, were ways of assessing the mood in Saladin's camp. Early in November, al-Adil entertained Richard in his tent for a day, serving him with the finest Turkish dishes and all manner of exotic delicacies. All this time, Conrad of Montferrat refused to give Richard any help. Indeed, he had told Saladin that he would break with the Crusaders if he were given Beirut and Sidon. But since he had, in effect, already broken with them, Saladin saw no reason to give away two valuable towns for nothing. Conrad would have to take up arms against Richard if his alliance was to be of any use to Saladin, and even Conrad did not dare to go quite as far as that.

Throughout November and December 1191, Richard concentrated on rebuilding the castles on the road from Jaffa to Jerusalem – castles which Saladin had dismantled. Saladin retreated to Jerusalem, contenting himself with sending out patrols to raid Richard's lines of communication and to attack any foraging parties which were not properly guarded. Despite the criticism of his more cautious advisers, Richard himself took part in many of the skirmishes. In these circumstances, the advance towards Jerusalem was necessarily slow. But by the end of the year the main body of the army was encamped at Beit Nuba, only twelve miles from the Holy City.

In the autumn of 1191, Richard I opened negotiations with Safadin, Saladin's brother, to make a truce. Matthew Paris has depicted the creating of a truce between Crusaders and Saracens in his *Chronica Majora*, though in this case the Crusader negotiator is Peter of Dreux, Count of Brittany.

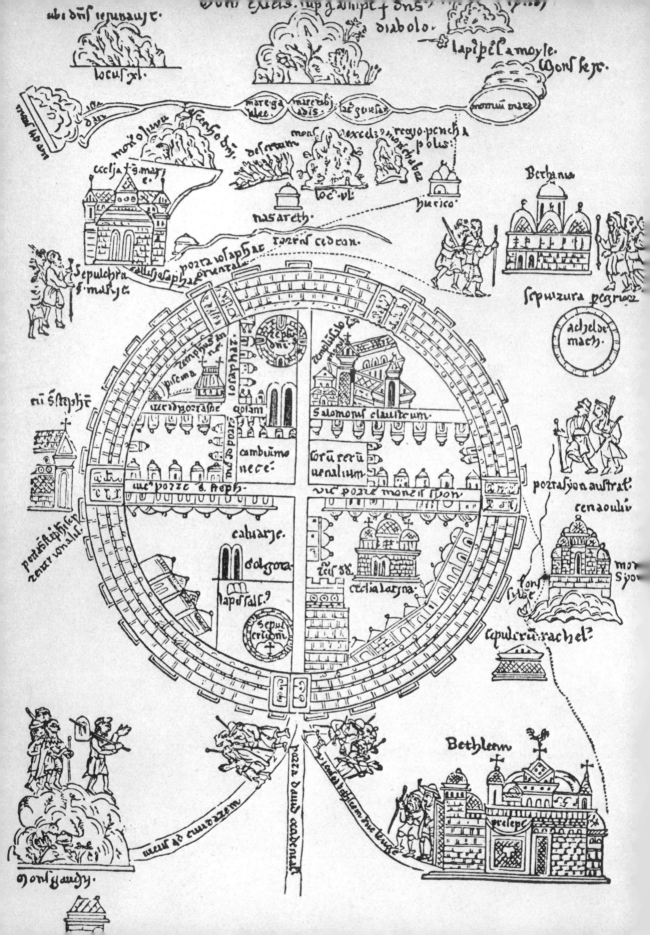

The weather was appalling; heavy rain and violent hail-storms; mud everywhere. Yet the soldiers were in jubilant mood, and they gave thanks to the God who had brought them so far:

OPPOSITE Twelfth-century plan of Jerusalem, produced by a Flemish artist.

> God may we now our voices raise
> In thanks, in worship and in praise!
> Now we shall see Thy Holy Tomb!'
> No man felt any grief or gloom,
> Or any sadness or distress,
> For all was joy and happiness.

But not everyone was so optimistic. Those who knew the country and who were sufficiently farsighted to see what would happen if Jerusalem were captured, took a wiser and sadder view. Foremost among these men were the Templars and Hospitallers. They pointed out that if Richard laid siege to Jerusalem, he would almost certainly be caught between the garrison and a relieving army. What hope was there of escaping from that trap when they were so far from the sea? And if they did take Jerusalem, what then? The enthusiastic Crusaders, who saw themselves as pilgrims to the Holy Sepulchre, would all go home, their pilgrimage completed, their vows fulfilled. How many could be persuaded to live in Jerusalem and defend it? As they could see, it was not exactly a land flowing with milk and honey. The answers to these questions were obvious. At a meeting of the army council held in January 1192, the inevitable decision was taken. Richard gave the order to retreat. To many of the ordinary soldiers, the pilgrims, it was a bitter blow. The weather conditions which had been bearable while they were marching forward to the Holy City, were now intolerable. Even the elements seemed to be mocking them:

> Every pilgrim cursed the day
> When he into the world was born. (Ambroise)

And to these men Richard, the conqueror of Cyprus and of Acre, the victor of Arsuf, was now the general who turned back from the gates of Jerusalem.

ne as me natt on net
Sad home enfitutice ke tão se eq p
kine quidaste il lui derainer

6 Crusaders and

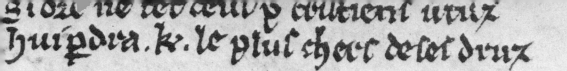

Assassins 1192-3

D ISHEARTENED, THE ARMY marched back from Beit Nuba, away from Jerusalem. The council which had voted to retreat had also decided that the most sensible course was to take Ascalon and rebuild it. This was sound military strategy, but it was not for this that many soldiers had crossed the sea. Hugh of Burgundy and most of the French contingents retired to Jaffa; some even to Acre. It was with a much diminished army that Richard reached Ascalon on 20 January 1192. For the next four months Richard's forces remained here, making it the strongest fortress on the coast of Palestine. They received no help from Conrad of Montferrat and precious little from anyone else. The Duke of Burgundy rejoined them for a while in early February, but then went back to Acre as soon as Richard announced that he could not afford to lend him any more money.

Acre was in chaos. Those old rivals the Pisans and the Genoese were once more at each other's throats. The Pisans, claiming to act on behalf of Guy of Lusignan, seized Acre and held it against the Genoese who were joined by Conrad of Montferrat and Hugh of Burgundy. The Pisans looked to Richard to support them against this coalition. Richard was on his way north to a conference with Conrad when he received their appeal for help. He reached Acre on 20 February to find that the news of his approach had forced Conrad and Hugh to

beat a hasty retreat to Tyre. Richard managed to bring about a temporary reconciliation between the Pisans and the Genoese; then he went north to see Conrad. The two men met at Casal Imbert on the road to Tyre. Conrad again refused to join the army at Ascalon and, on both sides, angry words were spoken. So the English had to bear the brunt of the war against Saladin, while the French enjoyed themselves at Tyre. Reliable sources kept Ambroise informed of their activities:

> Those who were present assured
> Us that they danced through the late hours
> Of night, their heads bedecked with flowers,
> Entwined in garland and in crown;
> Beside wine casks they sat them down
> And drank until matins had rung;
> Then homeward made their way among
> The harlots ...

Throughout March, Richard's men pressed on with the work at Ascalon. Simultaneously, Richard continued to negotiate with Saladin. Once he had drawn back from Jerusalem, there was a clear need for a settlement which would allow the Christian lords to rule the coastline in peace. It was time to consolidate the gains made in the last year.

From Richard's point of view, the need for peace became urgent as a result of news which reached him on 15 April. His brother John was making trouble in England and King Philip of France, unmindful of the oath he had sworn, was threatening the borders of Normandy. Richard would have to return to his ancestral lands. But what would happen in Outremer when he was gone? Despite the compromise worked out at Acre in the previous year Conrad was not prepared to co-operate with Guy of Lusignan. If the feud continued, Saladin would almost certainly be able to recover the ground he had lost in the last twelve months. The kingdom desperately needed a king who could rule effectively; whether or not he had a good legal claim to the crown was a matter of secondary importance. With this in mind, on 16 April Richard called a meeting of the army council at Ascalon – within twenty-four hours of the coming of the messenger from England. He gave the assembly a choice of kings: Conrad or Guy. Unanimously the council opted for

lef en douraffent

**Delantre denique fachiez quele fu
fonz leuefchie deni comede Aief tem**

One method of intimidating the garrison – besiegers catapulting the decapitated heads of prisoners into a beleagured city: from the thirteenth-century *Les Histoires d'Outremer*.

Conrad. It has always been said that this decision came as a shocking surprise to Richard, but this is hardly likely. It is true that up till now he had consistently taken Guy's side. In practice, however, this had simply meant that Richard had been King of Jerusalem, not Guy. If Richard had wanted Guy to take over the direction of affairs, there would have been no need to call a meeting of the army council and offer them a choice of kings. Richard's army already recognised a king, Guy, and to call a meeting made sense only if a policy change was being considered. Naturally Richard could not drop Guy without a single word of regret and so, very properly, he expressed his sorrow at what had happened before announcing that he would abide by the decision of the council. While Richard had been king in reality, Guy could perfectly well be king in theory, but now that he would have to come out from under Richard's shadow and stand on his own feet, it was clear that he would not do. Guy was an attractive man and a gallant soldier but, as everybody recognised, he was also a bit simple. Certainly, on his own, he had no hope of standing up to the clever and ruthless Conrad of Montferrat. In the eyes of the native barons

144

Conrad was the man who had saved Outremer by his heroic defence of Tyre; Guy was the man who had lost the Battle of Hattin. Richard was under no illusions. When he was gone, only a man like Conrad had the ability to face Saladin.

What then was to be Guy of Lusignan's fate? Fortunately Richard was in a position to compensate him in magnificent style. He made him Lord of Cyprus. Earlier, Richard had sold Cyprus to the Templars for one hundred thousand besants. So far they had paid only forty per cent of the purchase price and their attempt to raise the money by imposing a tax on the Greek Cypriot population had provoked a rebellion. It looked as though Cyprus was going to be more trouble than it was worth. Thus they were easily persuaded to sell out to Guy in return for forty thousand besants. Richard did not press Guy for payment of the balance of sixty thousand besants and it was, in fact, never paid. Guy's family, the Lusignans, were to rule Cyprus for the next three centuries, until 1489.

Meanwhile, Conrad of Montferrat had to be told of the army's choice. So Richard sent Count Henry of Champagne to Tyre. Count Henry was a distinguished Crusader who had been in the Holy Land for nearly two years. As the nephew of both King Richard and King Philip, he was in a good position to heal the divisions between the Angevin and French forces. For this reason, indeed, he had acted as commander of the army besieging Acre from the time of his arrival in the summer of 1190 until the coming of the two Kings in 1191. In the last few months he had become clearly aligned with Richard's party, preferring to remain at Ascalon rather than withdraw to Acre or Tyre. When Count Henry told him the news, Conrad of Montferrat fell on his knees and thanked God, asking that God should not permit him to be crowned if he were not worthy to be king. There was great urgency, so it was agreed that Conrad should be crowned at Acre within the next few days. Count Henry left, in order to make preparations for the coronation. But no one had reckoned with the assassin's knife.

On 28 April Conrad had expected to dine at home with his wife Isabella. She, however, took so long over her bath that he eventually gave up and went round to the house of his friend the Bishop of Beauvais, in the hope of dining there. Unfortunately, the bishop had just finished his dinner so – doubtless reflecting that it was not his lucky day – Conrad headed home again. Turning a corner, he was met by two monks, one of whom seemed to have a letter for him. As Conrad went to take the letter they stabbed him. Mortally wounded, Conrad was carried back to the palace. A politician to the last, he commanded Isabella to give the keys of Tyre to no one but Richard or the duly elected King of Jerusalem.

Who were the killers? And why had they chosen to kill Conrad? Before he was executed, one of them confessed that they had disguised themselves as monks in order to worm their way into Conrad's confidence. In reality, they were both followers of Rashid ed-Din Sinan, a legendary figure in the Near East and popularly known as 'The Old Man of the Mountains'. From 1169 until his death in 1193 Rashid was the leader of the Syrian branch of a revolutionary religious movement which had been founded in Persia at the end of the eleventh century. The orthodox Muslims who ruled Persia looked upon the followers of the new teaching as heretics and tried to suppress them. But these heretics did not submit meekly to persecution. They created a secure base for themselves in the great mountain fortress of Alamut, and they struck back at those who attacked them. Their chosen weapon was the assassin's dagger. In the early twelfth century the new teaching, together with its terrorist techniques, was carried into Syria and it was here that its devotees were given the name by which they are remembered: they were called the 'Assassins'. The word 'assassin' comes from the Arabic *hashish*. Their enemies accused them of taking hashish. To outsiders it seemed the easiest way of explaining

Crusader besant, with Arabic lettering. The besant was a gold coin which derived its name from Byzantium, the Empire of the East.

why they acted the way they did. In fact, there is no good evidence to prove that they really did take hashish, but there is no doubt at all about the fact that they used murder as a political weapon. Thus, in the course of the twelfth and thirteenth centuries, a new word entered the languages of Europe: assassin, a professional killer.

The description of the Assassins given by the late twelfth-century German chronicler Arnold of Lübeck, illustrates very well the impact which the Old Man of the Mountains made on the European imagination:

> This Old Man has by his witchcraft so bemused the men of his country that they neither worship nor believe in any God but him. He entices them with promises of an after life in which they will enjoy eternal pleasure and so he makes them prefer death to life. He only has to give the nod and they will jump off a high wall, breaking their skulls and dying miserably. The truly blessed so he tells them, are those who kill others and are themselves killed. Whenever any of his followers choose to die in this way, he presents them with knives which are, so to speak, consecrated to murder. He then gives them a potion which intoxicates them, plunging them into ecstasy and oblivion. Thus he uses his magic to make them see fantastic dreams, full of pleasures and delights. He promises them that they will live in such dreams for ever if they die when killing at his command.

Because many of their deeds were done by stealth, the power of the Assassins was easily magnified. There was no way of knowing where they would strike next. A story involving Saladin tells us much about the nature of the power attributed to Rashid ed-Din. According to this tale the Old Man of the Mountains sent a messenger to Saladin with instructions to deliver the message only in private. Naturally Saladin had the messenger searched, but no weapon was found. Then Saladin dismissed everyone but a few trusted advisers. The messenger refused, however, to deliver his message. So Saladin sent everyone away except his two personal bodyguards. Still the messenger was reluctant, but Saladin said: 'These two never leave my side. I look upon them as my sons. Deliver your message or not, as you choose.' Then the messenger turned to the two bodyguards and said: 'If I ordered you in the name of my master to kill Saladin, would you do so?' They said they would, and

OVERLEAF Assassins killing Nizam al-Mulk, from an early fourteenth-century Persian manuscript of the *Jami al-tavarikh* of Rashid ed-Din Sinan, 'the Old Man of the Mountains'.

147

drew their swords, saying, 'Command us as you wish.' The messenger ordered them to sheathe their swords and all three now left the Sultan's camp. Saladin was dumb-founded, as well he might be. But Rashid ed-Din Sinan's message had been delivered. We have to remember that Saladin was the champion of Muslim orthodoxy and he was therefore in greater danger of assassination than were most Christians. There were, indeed, at least two attempts on his life.

But why should the Assassins have wanted to murder Conrad of Montferrat? Nobody really knew the answer to this and all kinds of rumours spread rapidly. Some said that Saladin had bribed Rashid to kill both Conrad and Richard, but Sinan would kill only one of them since he knew that, with both out of the way, the Sultan would have a free hand to deal with the Assassins. Others blamed Richard; indeed the Assassin's own confession was said to have implicated the King of England. But even if such a confession were made, it would not be very reliable evidence. It was a normal part of the Assassins' technique to provide the murderer with a 'cover story' of this kind in order to spread mistrust and suspicion in the opposing camp. Richard was the obvious man for the Assassins to implicate. He and Conrad had always been political enemies, and an observer, even if he had heard the news of the recent reconciliation between them, might well have thought that there was something suspicious about so complete a reversal of Richard's attitude. Only someone who understood the situation in England and Normandy could make sense of Richard's sudden switch. There were many French Crusaders who were prepared to believe anything that was said against Richard, particularly when it became clear that the man who had most obviously gained from Conrad's death was Richard's nephew, Henry of Champagne. Fortunately for Richard, however, he was explicitly cleared of the charge in a letter written by the Old Man of the Mountains himself and sent to Leopold of Austria. At least, the letter was intended to look as though it had been written by Rashid. In fact it was a forgery. Someone in the English camp was attempting to dispel the rumours.

At this distance in time, it is no easier than it was then to know what really lay behind the murder of Conrad. Everything we know about Saladin and Richard, however, suggests that they would not have stooped to assassination. Interestingly enough, the sources which were closest to Conrad, the chronicles which reflect neither the French nor the English nor the Muslim point of view, but rather that of the native baronage of Outremer, simply say that Conrad had offended Rashid by an act of piracy and that this was the Old Man's revenge. It was not the kind of explanation to appeal to amateur politicians. It was far too simple for that. They preferred to look for deeper causes and for plots of Machiavellian subtlety. Nonetheless, on the evidence available, it seems that this is probably what happened.

When Henry of Champagne, in Acre, heard the shocking news he at once hurried back to Tyre. Isabella had shut herself up in the castle and, following her dead husband's instructions, she had refused to hand over the keys of the city to the Duke of

Brass canteen, inlaid with silver, made in Damascus in the mid-thirteenth century.

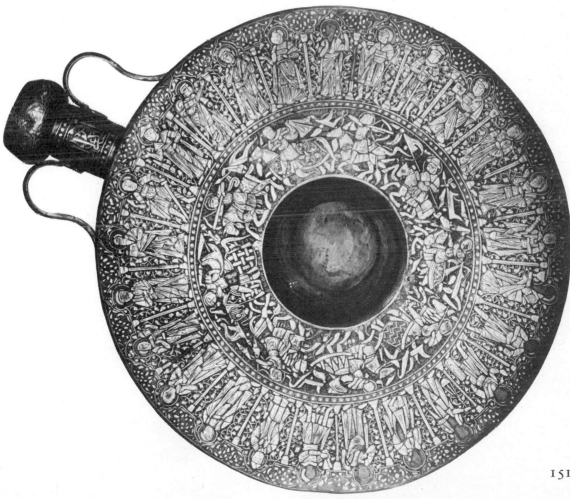

The Crusader chapel in the castle of Krak des Chevaliers in Syria.

Burgundy. But she could not stay there forever. If Jerusalem was to have a king, then Isabella, the twenty-one-year-old, twice-married heiress to the kingdom, had to find a third husband. Count Henry's arrival in Tyre seemed to offer a heaven-sent solution to the problem. Henry was a bachelor; he was young, brave and popular. With his royal connexions in both England and France he was the ideal man to end the struggle of the factions in Outremer. Isabella yielded to popular demand and offered herself and the keys of the city to Henry. Henry was cautious. He would not act until he had obtained Richard's consent. Needless to say, Richard gave his approval. He was not sure if the marriage would be legally valid, but he was glad to see his nephew chosen King of Jerusalem. At Acre, on 5 May, after one week of widowhood, Isabella married Henry amid general rejoicing. Once again Ambroise reflects the prevailing mood.

> The French delayed not in the least
> But sent straightway to fetch the priest
> And caused the count to wed the dame.
> My soul, I should have done the same,
> For she was fair and beautiful.

After the wedding Henry and Isabella were installed in the royal palace:

> The count is richly lodged. Ah, would
> That I had anything so good.

Saladin's secretary took a less romantic view:

> Count Henry became lord of Tyre and married Conrad's wife on the same night, maintaining that he had first right to the dead man's wife. She was pregnant, but this did not prevent his uniting himself with her, something even more disgusting than the coupling of the flesh. I asked one of their courtiers to whom paternity would be awarded and he said: 'It will be the Queen's child.' You see the licentiousness of these foul unbelievers.

In the last twenty days, events had moved with bewildering speed. On 15 April Guy had still been King of Jerusalem. By 5 May he was Lord of Cyprus, while the kingdom of Jerusalem was already welcoming its third ruler in as many weeks. Oddly enough, Henry never assumed the title of King, perhaps because he could not be crowned in Jerusalem. After the departure of King Richard, however, he became the effective ruler of the kingdom until 1197, when he accidentally stepped backwards through the open window of an upper room and was killed. Isabella then married, as her fourth husband, Guy of Lusignan's brother Amalric, who died of a surfeit of fish in 1205. Thus, by the time she was thirty-three, Isabella had been divorced once and widowed three times. When she herself died soon afterwards, the world must have seemed a safer place for husbands.

OVERLEAF Aerial view of Krak des Chevaliers, the great Crusader fortress which lies in the Nusairi mountains of southern Syria. The earliest surviving portion is the inner ward, built between 1140–1200. The defensive plan consists of two concentric lines of fortifications, studded where necessary by powerful towers.

153

From Richard's point of view, the accession of Henry of Champagne meant that, for the first time, he had all the forces of the kingdom at his disposal. He decided to seize the opportunity to add to the length of the coastline in Christian hands. Summoning Henry and the French army to join him, he ordered an attack on the fortress of Darum, twenty miles south of Ascalon. In fact, after five days of fierce fighting, Darum fell on 22 May, one day before Henry and the Duke of Burgundy arrived. But, in a fine gesture, Richard at once handed the captured town to the new Lord of Jerusalem. Encouraged by this, the united army pressed for an immediate march on Jerusalem. Now that there was a new spirit of co-operation among the Christians they would surely succeed. This time, moreover, they would not be hampered by the winter rain and mud.

Richard was now caught in a terrible dilemma, reinforced by the arrival of another messenger from England with more disquieting news about the conspiracy between John and Philip Augustus. Which was the higher cause, which the more urgent problem – Jerusalem or the Angevin Empire? It would have taken the messenger about eight weeks to travel from London to Ascalon. What had happened in those weeks? Was the situation worse or better? Jerusalem at least was near at hand. Should he try again to take it? It was a forlorn hope, if ever there was one, but did he want to be known as the King who did not even try? And if by some miracle he took Jerusalem there would be no one in Europe who could stand against him, the conqueror who had restored the Holy City to Christendom. But suppose he failed and returned home too late?

Under the strain, Richard seems to have suffered a nervous collapse. For several days he stayed in his tent, alone and despondent, while all around him the army rejoiced at the prospect of marching to Jerusalem. Finally, one of his chaplains, William of Poitou, managed to talk to him and revive his spirits. He reminded the King of all the past triumphs which God had allowed him to enjoy, all the dangers which he had, by God's grace, escaped. Now that he had been brought to the verge of the ultimate victory, it would be a shameful thing to retreat. 'All agree, O King, that you are the father, the champion and the defender of Christendom. If you desert God's people now they will be destroyed by the enemy.' William had found the

Crusaders attacking a town by breaking down its city gates with an axe, from the thirteenth-century *Les Histoires d'Outremer*.

right note. Richard made up his mind. He announced that he would stay in Palestine till the following Easter and that all should at once prepare for the siege of Jerusalem.

On 7 June the army, in cheerful mood, marched out of Ascalon. Four days later they reached Beit Nuba without encountering any opposition. Their only losses were two soldiers who died from snake bites. Saladin, at Jerusalem, waited for them. At Beit Nuba, however, the army was once again brought up against the realities of the situation. They were back where they had been six months earlier. Nothing had changed. To besiege Jerusalem was to court disaster. Emotionally, however, it was very difficult to come to terms with this hard fact. For three weeks the Crusaders hesitated. They even achieved a resounding success in ambushing a rich caravan and capturing an immense amount of booty, including

157

some thousands of horses and camels. Ambroise found the meat
of a young camel very tasty:

> They have a white and savoury flesh
> When larded well and roasted fresh.

Equally morale-boosting was the convenient discovery that
two separate fragments of the Holy Cross had somehow
escaped capture in 1187. One piece was brought into the camp
by a local Syrian bishop. A few days later the abbot of the Greek
monastery of Mar Elias – according to Ambroise his face was
the very picture of holiness – revealed to Richard that he had
buried a second fragment in order to prevent it falling into
infidel hands. The Crusaders dug in the spot pointed out to
them and found what they were looking for. All this was some
consolation; nonetheless there were bitter words spoken when,
for the second time, Richard gave the inevitable order for
retreat. According to one of his admirers, Richard had offered
to go to Jerusalem if the army insisted on it, but he would not
lead them there; he would go as their comrade, their fellow-
pilgrim, but not as their commander. He refused to lead them
into a trap. Already Saladin was attacking the supply line to
Jaffa. But opinion in the army was divided, with only the
French under Hugh of Burgundy insisting that they should
besiege Jerusalem, whatever the odds against them might be.
An alternative plan of attack, an advance on Cairo, made much
better strategic sense, since if they could only weaken Saladin's
hold on the rich resources of Egypt, there was a chance of for-
cing him to abandon Jerusalem. This, in fact, was precisely the
line of approach used by the Crusaders of the thirteenth
century.

But the French would have nothing to do with this scheme.
For them it was Jerusalem or nothing, and so, inevitably, it
was nothing. The tension in the camp was not eased when the
French troops began to sing an insulting song about Richard,
which had been composed by the Duke of Burgundy. Richard,
the troubadour, naturally replied in a similar vein. Unfortunately the texts of the two songs do not survive. On 4 July the
withdrawal began. For Richard, it must have been a day of
misery. After all, in agreeing to try once more, he had risked
far more than the rest. He had failed to win Jerusalem but he

'*His face was
the very picture
of holiness*'

might yet have succeeded in throwing away the Angevin Empire. It is said that one day while the army was encamped at Beit Nuba, Richard went out riding over the hills near Emmaus. Suddenly he caught a glimpse of the walls and the towers of Jerusalem on the horizon. Hastily he covered his face with his shield, for he did not want to see the city which he could not deliver. More than half a century later, when the French King Louis IX – Saint Louis – was in Palestine, his advisers reminded him of this story. It was, they said, no disgrace to Louis that he could not save Jerusalem, when it had been beyond the strength of even the greatest of all Christian kings.

By various routes, the army returned to the coast. Richard re-opened negotiations with Saladin and they were quickly able to come very close to a settlement. Saladin agreed to allow pilgrims into Jerusalem and to cede the coast to the Christians, provided that they demolish Ascalon. Richard, however, refused to consider the demolition of a fortress on which he had spent so much time and money. While the argument about Ascalon was still going on, Richard moved to Acre. He may have intended to march on Beirut, seize it and then embark for Europe, even though no peace treaty had yet been sealed. But Saladin moved first. On 27 July, the day after Richard arrived in Acre, his army appeared outside the walls of Jaffa. After resisting bravely for three days, the town surrendered. On payment of a ransom Saladin was prepared to allow the Christians to leave Jaffa with their goods. Unfortunately, the years of non-stop campaigning had had their effect on Saladin's troops. They were exhausted and mutinous; only the prospect of sacking Jaffa had kept them going and they did not intend to be deprived of their plunder. They swept through the town, looting and killing, so Saladin advised the defenders to retreat to the citadel and stay there until he had regained control.

Meanwhile, on 29 July, Richard heard the news. He at once ordered Henry of Champagne to lead the army south, while he himself, with a handful of knights and crossbowmen, went aboard his galleys. The winds were against them and they did not reach Jaffa until 31 July. To their dismay, they could see Saladin's banners waving over the town. Inside Jaffa Saladin had restored order and the Christians were just beginning to file out of the citadel when they saw Richard's fleet approaching. They at once took up arms again. Richard, however, had no idea what was happening in Jaffa and hesitated. Then a priest climbed down the walls of the citadel onto the beach and swam out to the galleys. As soon as Richard knew that the citadel was still holding out, he brought his galleys in close to the beach. Leaving off some of his armour in the interests of rapid movement, Richard plunged into the shallow water and waded ashore, followed by his men. Supported by a sally from the garrison of the citadel, he quickly drove the enemy out of Jaffa. The Turks, in complete confusion, uncertain as to whether the garrison had or had not surrendered, never really knew what hit them.

Saladin withdrew about five miles inland and at once resumed peace negotiations. As before, Ascalon proved to be a stumbling block. Saladin therefore decided to try a surprise attack on Richard before his main army had time to link up with the amphibious force. Owing to the stench of dead bodies inside Jaffa, Richard had made his camp outside the town walls, which had, in any case, been badly damaged by Saladin's mines and siege machines. During the night of 4 August, the Turkish cavalry moved quietly forward. But Richard received just enough warning of their approach to be able to get the troops into battle array, though some of his soldiers were apparently only half-dressed. In the eyes of his followers, the day was won for them by Richard's individual prowess:

> The King was a giant in the battle and was everywhere in the field, now here, now there, wherever the attacks of the Turks raged most fiercely. On that day his sword shone like lightning and many of the Turks felt its edge. Some were cloven in two from their helmet to their teeth; others lost their heads, arms and other limbs, lopped off at a single blow. He mowed men down as reapers mow down the corn with their sickles. Whoever felt one of his blows had no need of a second.

Achilles, Alexander, Roland – none of the heroes of the past could have performed greater deeds than he did that day. It was in such terms as these that Richard's admirers wrote about him. In reality, it seems that the Turks rather lost interest in the battle once they realised that they had lost the advantage of surprise.

OPPOSITE 'Wheel' map of the world, with Jerusalem in the centre, from a thirteenth-century English psalter.

160

Some indeed reminded Saladin that he had tried to rob them of the pleasure of sacking Jaffa, and simply refused to attack. But their reluctance indicates that Richard was still reaping the psychological rewards of his victory at Arsuf.

Both sides were now completely worn out. Richard himself fell seriously ill. (It was said that he began to recover from the moment when he heard that Hugh of Burgundy had died at Acre.) It was time to make peace and go home. Richard did his best to save Ascalon but it was no good. Saladin was adamant. It threatened his communications with Egypt, and it had to be in his possession. Eventually Richard gave way. The fortifications of Ascalon were razed to the ground and the town was then restored to Saladin. It was, in any event, clear that once Richard was gone the Christians of Outremer would not have been able to hold Ascalon if Saladin were really determined to take it. On 2 September, Saladin's and Richard's representatives agreed on the terms of a three-years' truce. From Tyre to Jaffa, the coast was to remain in Christian hands. Jerusalem, of course, was kept by the Muslims, but pilgrims were free to visit the city. Many of his followers took advantage of this opportunity but Richard did not. He would enter Jerusalem as a conqueror, but not on conditions laid down by unbelievers. Instead he travelled to Acre and made arrangements to leave. On 9 October 1192 he set sail. The Third Crusade – his Crusade – was over. In that it had not taken Jerusalem, it was a failure, but given the problems with which Richard and his fellow-commanders had to cope, it is amazing that they achieved as much as they did. Certainly Saladin feared that the coastal towns which the Franks now held might later be used as bases from which the rest of Palestine would be conquered. While Saladin was alive, there was not much chance of this, but after the great Muslim leader was gone, who could tell? Saladin himself had grave misgivings about the future of his people. Had Richard stayed in the Holy Land until the next Easter – as he had said he would – he might have achieved his ambition, for, by one of the ironies of history, Saladin died on 4 March 1193, more than three weeks before Easter. But by that time Richard was a prisoner in Germany.

7
Prisoner in

Germany 1193-4

'AS THE EARTH GROWS DARK when the sun goes down, so the face of the kingdom was changed by the absence of the King. All the barons were disturbed, castles were strengthened, towns fortified and ditches dug.' In these words the sharp-tongued chronicler Richard of Devizes summed up the state of English politics after Richard's departure for the Holy Land in the summer of 1190. The King had left the Bishop of Ely, William Longchamp, in charge of England. As Justiciar, it was his job to look after the whole machinery of government in the King's absence. Since he also held the offices of Chancellor and Papal Legate, he was supreme in Church and State. Richard knew him well. He was an old and trusted servant from the days when Richard was Count of Poitou. He was efficient, hard-working and unwaveringly loyal to the King. In many ways he appeared to be an excellent choice. Yet he proved unable to govern the country.

PREVIOUS PAGES The town of Dürnstein overlooked by its castle, where Richard I was held captive by Duke Leopold of Austria in 1193.

RIGHT Dover Castle, the great Norman stronghold built by William the Conqueror. The Constable of Dover became one of the leading men of the kingdom while the King was abroad, for he held the gateway to England. During the 1190s William Longchamp's brother-in-law was Constable of Dover.

In part this was the consequence of Longchamp's own short-comings. In appearance and in personality he seems to have been a cartoonist's dream. His enemies – and he had many – described him as small, ugly and with a taste for boys. Undoubtedly he had a gift for making himself unpopular. A cool judge of character wrote that lay people found him more than a king, the clergy more than a pope and both an intolerable tyrant. But Richard was also to blame. He had originally intended to banish his brother John, as he had banished Geoffrey, for three years, but at the last minute – at Eleanor's request – he relented and allowed John to enter England as and when he pleased. This created an impossible political situation. John's power, ambition and crookedness made him a trouble-maker whom no one minister could control. Eleanor might have been able to hold her son in check but she went to Spain to fetch Berengaria of Navarre and then on to Sicily. Once

Longchamp lost the support of his government colleagues he was bound to be overthrown.

By February 1191 Richard, in Sicily, had heard various reports of the unrest in England. He sent back Walter of Coutances, Archbishop of Rouen, with instructions to hold the balance between John and Longchamp. This worked for a while, but then Longchamp's agents made a bad mistake. Geoffrey, now consecrated Archbishop of York, decided to return to England to take over the duties of his see. He landed at Dover where Longchamp's brother-in-law was the constable of the castle. Learning that the constable's men intended to arrest him, he took refuge in St Martin's Priory. Here he was besieged for four days and then, on 18 September 1191, the constable's men went in after him and dragged him from the altar of the chapel. This act of violence reminded men of the death of Thomas Becket, with Longchamp in the part of Henry II. John and his propagandists had no difficulty in stirring up such strong feelings against the Justiciar that he was forced to leave the country in ignominy. The scene on Dover beach as Longchamp in disguise looked desperately for a boat in which he could cross the Channel is best left in the immortal, if unreliable, words of Hugh Nonant, John's chief propagandist and, in his spare time, Bishop of Coventry:

> Pretending to be a woman – a sex which he always hated – he changed his priest's robe into a harlot's dress. The shame of it! The man became a woman, the bishop a buffoon. Dressed in a green gown of enormous length he hurriedly limped – for the poor fellow was lame – from the castle heights down to the seashore and then sat down to rest on a rock. There he attracted the attention of a half-naked fisherman who was wet and cold from the sea and who thought the bishop was the sort of woman who might warm him up. He put his left arm around Longchamp's neck while his right hand roamed lower down. Suddenly pulling up the gown he plunged unblushingly in – only to be confronted with the irrefutable evidence that the woman was a man. The fisherman then called to his mates to come and see what he had found. Thoroughly alarmed by the ensuing commotion Longchamp's servants hastened to rescue their master.

Eventually, however, Longchamp's disguise landed him in difficulties from which his servants were unable to save him and

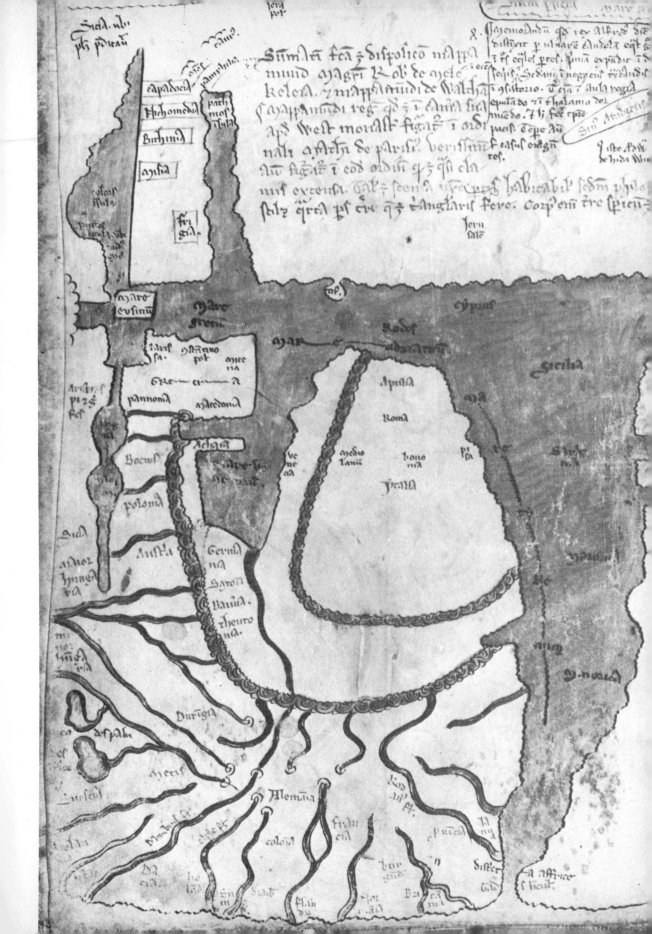

he was left to cool his heels in gaol for a week, before being released and finding his way to Flanders.

Much to John's disappointment, Longchamp's place at the head of the administration was taken by Walter of Coutances. But then Eleanor of Aquitaine returned, and she was just about able to hold her discontented son in check until the day when the whole political situation was put into the melting pot by the news that Richard had been captured by his bitter enemy, Leopold of Austria, and was even now lying in a German prison from which he might never escape.

A few days after leaving Acre Richard's fleet had been caught in a storm. Richard's galley, the *Franche-Nef*, lost contact with the other ships. Apart from a report that the *Franche-Nef* had been sighted off Brindisi there was no reliable news about Richard until early in January 1193. For nearly three months he seemed to have vanished from the face of the earth. The most likely explanation of his disappearance was that he had been drowned.

Later on, Anselm the chaplain, one of his companions on that strange journey into captivity, gave a full account of what had happened. At first all went reasonably well, and Richard was nearing Marseilles when he learned that Count Raymond of Toulouse intended to seize him as soon as he landed. For there was constant war between the Counts of Poitou and Toulouse, and only a few months earlier, Richard's Seneschal of Gascony had carried out a destructive raid right up to the gates of Toulouse itself. If Raymond captured him, Richard knew that he would be handed over to the tender mercies of Philip Augustus. The obvious course of action was to steer for the Straits of Gibraltar, but contrary winds made this impossible. In order to avoid having to travel through lands under Philip's overlordship, Richard decided to return home via Germany. He set sail for the Adriatic. Near Corfu, the *Franche-Nef* was set upon by pirates. They were beaten off but Richard was attracted to their bold fighting spirit and came to terms with them. The *Franche-Nef* had been badly battered by rough seas. Richard needed another ship, so he offered to pay the pirates well if they would give him and his followers – now disguised as pilgrims – passage to the north shore of the Adriatic Sea. The deal was closed and

OPPOSITE Henry VI, the Emperor and King of Germany. A miniature from a version of the *Manessischen Liederhandschrift*.

171

Richard transferred to the pirate ship. As they approached their destination, another storm struck. Somewhere between Venice and Aquileia their ship was driven ashore and wrecked. Richard was now in the territory of the German Emperor, Henry VI. From here the direct route home would have been through Verona to the Brenner, then through the Tirol and Swabia to the River Rhine. But this route would have taken Richard right into the centre of Henry VI's power, and the two sovereigns were hardly on friendly terms. In autumn 1191, while Richard was in Sicily, he had made an alliance with King Tancred against Henry. In the unlikely event of the fierce German King having forgotten this, he would have been reminded of it by Philip of France when they met in Italy during Philip's journey home from Acre. But Richard was sufficiently well-informed about German politics to know that if he headed north-east, towards Bohemia, he would reach the lands ruled by a group of princes who were hostile to Henry VI. The key figures in this group were the Welf (or Guelf) family, and the greatest of the Welfs was Richard's brother-in-law, Henry the Lion, formerly Duke of both Saxony and Bavaria. Once Richard had reached Bohemia or Moravia he would be able to travel on roads controlled by his kinsmen and their allies until he reached a Baltic or a North Sea port. Moreover, in midwinter, with snow thick on the ground, the passes in the central Alps were very difficult, while the road to Bohemia led to the Pontebba Pass over a fairly low range. The disadvantage of this route was that it would take him through the lands belonging to Count Meinhard of Görz – a kinsman of Conrad of Montferrat – and then into Austria. But if he could evade Duke Leopold's clutches he would almost certainly be safe for the rest of the way home. Richard decided to take the risk.

He would travel disguised as a merchant, one of a party of pilgrims returning from the Holy Land. Almost at once, however, the suspicions of the local magnates were aroused. Anyone who was curious about the fate of the English King was sure to investigate thoroughly reports that a group of English pilgrims had been seen in the vicinity. And when these pilgrims spent money on a truly royal scale it was unlikely that anyone would be deceived by their attempted disguise. A German chronicler says that when Richard was captured he was found roasting

OPPOSITE The monuments of Henry the Lion and Matilda in Brunswick Cathedral. Henry the Lion was Duke of Saxony and Bavaria and a member of the family of Welf. In 1168 he married Matilda, daughter of Henry II of England, and Richard's sister.

meat on a spit, hoping that by doing this servile work he would avoid recognition. Unfortunately the kitchen servant was still wearing a magnificent ring, worth several years' wages. The details of this story are probably not true, but it captures the spirit of the whole affair. At Friesach in Carinthia, Richard had a lucky escape when the local lord sent one of his household to inspect the newly arrived pilgrims. But this man, although he had lived in Carinthia for twenty years, was by birth a Norman and when he saw Richard, whom he instantly recognised, he went down on his knees before him and burst into tears. He then provided fresh horses for Richard and two others whom he advised to ride north as fast as possible, leaving the rest of the party behind to act as a decoy. After three days' and three nights' hard riding, Richard and his companions had reached Vienna – less than fifty miles from the safety of the Moravian border. But Richard was so exhausted that they were forced to rest at an inn just outside the city. Once again they spent money too freely and this time there was no Norman to rescue them. Here, shortly before Christmas 1192, Richard fell into the hands of Leopold of Austria. After this time no one in England had a kind word for the Austrians: 'they are savages who live more like wild beasts than men' wrote one chronicler.

Leopold sent Richard to a strong castle built high on a mountain-slope overlooking the Danube: the castle of Dürn-stein. The castle is in ruins today, but a legend still clings to its broken walls, the legend of Blondel, the faithful minstrel who travelled the length and breadth of Germany in search of his missing lord. He visited castle after castle and outside each one sang the first lines of a song which he and Richard had composed together. At last, at Dürnstein, he heard the refrain. In its earliest known form, the legend was told by a Rheims minstrel in the second half of the thirteenth century. There is not a shred of evidence to indicate that there is any truth in the story – but it was, at least, good publicity for minstrels. As soon as Henry VI heard the news, he summoned Duke Leopold to bring Richard to him. The bargaining was about to begin.

For more than a year kings and princes haggled over Richard's body – the body of a man who was a Crusader and supposedly, therefore, under the protection of the Church. But in the eyes of politicians, the most valuable piece on the chess-

Richard's Route into Captivity

board of Europe had been captured and the bidding for him was correspondingly fierce. Events in the Byzantine Empire and Sicily, as well as in England, France and Germany, depended upon the outcome of the auction. The first deal to be negotiated was the sale of Richard to Henry VI. This was done in February 1193. Out of the total of one hundred thousand marks which was, in effect, the reserve price placed on Richard's head, it was agreed that Leopold should have seventy-five thousand marks. Fifty thousand marks of this were disguised as a dowry for Eleanor of Brittany, Richard's niece, who was to marry one of

Leopold's sons. In addition, Richard was to release, without ransom, the prisoners he had taken in Cyprus, Isaac Comnenus and his daughter, and the island was to be restored to them. On his mother's side, Leopold was related to Isaac and he intended to right the wrongs done to his kinsman. In fact, although Cyprus remained firmly in the hands of the Lusignan family, Leopold was able to secure Isaac's liberation. No sooner was he out of prison than he made a bid to seize the throne of Constantinople. But sudden death – he may have been poisoned – put an end to Isaac's hopes of a new empire. Leopold

The castle of Dürnstein overlooking the Danube, where Leopold imprisoned Richard I.

and Henry VI also agreed that Richard should come with fifty galleys and two hundred knights to assist the German King on his next invasion of Sicily. All this had been a matter for Henry VI and Leopold to settle; Richard himself had no say in any of it.

By now, of course, all of Christendom knew that Richard was a prisoner somewhere in Germany. Philip of France had been told the news by Henry VI himself: 'Inasmuch as he is now in our power and has always done his utmost to annoy and disturb you, we have thought it right to notify your highness, for we know that these tidings will bring you most abundant joy.' Philip passed the information on to the man he believed could make the best use of it. By mid-January 1193, Count John was on his way to France. At Paris he did homage to Philip for Normandy and all of Richard's other lands, including – or so it was believed in England – even England. He promised to marry Alice, the lady whom Richard had discarded, and to hand over Gisors and the Norman Vexin to Philip. He then returned to England to stir up rebellion, asking the Welsh and the Scots to give him aid. William, King of the Scots, would have nothing to do with such treacherous schemes, but John was able to hire some Welsh mercenaries and garrison the key Thames Valley castles of Wallingford and Windsor. He then claimed to be king, asserting that his brother Richard was dead. A few believed him, but Queen Eleanor, the Justiciars and the barons knew John, and they did not.

Meanwhile, a copy of Henry VI's letter to Philip had come into the hands of Walter of Coutances. He summoned the great council of the realm to a meeting on 28 February 1193. The council decided to send two abbots to Germany in the hope of discovering Richard's exact whereabouts. Late in March, they found Richard at Ochsenfurt, a small town on the River Main not far from Würzburg. He was being taken to Speyer to answer the charges brought against him by Henry VI and Duke Leopold.

Richard greeted the two abbots warmly. They were the first visitors able to give him reliable information on recent events in England and Normandy, so he questioned them closely. Although he grieved over his brother's disloyalty, a poor return for all the favours and gifts he had showered upon him, he consoled himself with the thought that John was not the

Minstrels and Troubadours

The word minstrel is derived from the Latin, *Minister*, and was used in the twelfth and thirteenth centuries to signify a Court musician entertainer. The term covers a great variety of performers, but at the head of the profession stood the troubadour, who was often a figure of high social standing. A ruler's prestige was enhanced if he could attract the best troubadours to his Court. Blondel, minstrel to Richard I, is said to have travelled around Germany in search of his lost master. Outside each castle he sang one line of a song he had composed with Richard, until at last he found the King imprisoned in Dürnstein. Even if this legend is not true, it shows that popular opinion saw in Richard a king who enjoyed music and poetry.

Illustrations from a thirteenth-century edition of the *Manessischen Liederhandschrift*, showing various famous troubadours:
RIGHT Bruno von Hornberg.
BELOW LEFT Christian von Hamle.
BELOW RIGHT Conrad von Altstettin.
OPPOSITE Brunvart von Ougheim.

man to take a country if there was anyone at all to resist him.

The abbots accompanied Richard on the last three days of his journey to Speyer. During this difficult time, his conduct won the admiration of all who met him; courteous, dignified even in captivity, self-possessed and able to rise above the vicissitudes of fortune, a man born to command. At Speyer, Richard had to undergo the ordeal of being, in effect, put in the dock. He was forced to listen to accusations that he had conspired against the Empire by allying with Henry VI's enemies, Tancred of Sicily and Henry the Lion; that he had ill-treated Leopold of Austria and plotted the death of Conrad of Montferrat. (One of Henry VI's most loyal supporters was Conrad's brother, Boniface of Montferrat.) When Richard's turn came, he replied so persuasively that, instead of blaming him, the Emperor praised him and gave him the kiss of peace. He also

A nineteenth-century impression of Richard I at Speyer, pleading his case before the Emperor Henry. The artist has portrayed the moment when Richard defended his actions so persuasively that the Emperor praised him and gave him the kiss of peace.

promised to bring about a reconciliation between Richard and Philip. This scene moved the onlookers to weep with joy. But, kiss or no kiss, Richard had to pay for his freedom. The sum required was one hundred thousand marks, and at a later meeting it was agreed that not until seventy thousand had actually been handed over would Richard be released. In addition, Richard was to supply Henry with fifty galleys and two hundred knights for a year. Then envoys from Philip were given a hearing. On behalf of their lord, they defied Richard, that is they declared that all ties of friendship between the Kings of France and England were now at an end. But when they returned to Philip, they took back with them a warning from Henry VI: whoever attacked Richard would find that he had also offended the Emperor. Henry VI's great ambition was to win Sicily, and he looked upon Richard's money and supplies as the means by which he would achieve this end.

At this crucial conference at Speyer on 21–22 March 1193 Richard was much comforted by the presence of his most brilliant adviser, Hubert Walter, Bishop of Salisbury. Hubert had gone to Outremer with Baldwin of Canterbury and, after the Archbishop's death on 19 November 1190, he had remained in charge of the English contingent at the siege of Acre until the arrival of Richard himself. From then on, he had been the King's inseparable companion in the Holy Land and had won a great reputation as a diplomat, soldier and administrator. On his way home from Acre he called in at Sicily and there he had heard the news of Richard's capture. Stopping only to enlist the aid of the Pope, now Celestine III, he had raced northwards to rejoin the King. Richard showed his gratitude and his good judgment by writing to his mother at once and asking her to see that Hubert was elected to the Archbishopric of Canterbury, which had remained vacant ever since Baldwin's death. Hubert Walter and the two abbots then took their leave and headed for England. Richard was sent to the castle of Trifels in the mountains west of Speyer. Apparently he was still in good spirits. 'He was cheerful and talkative. He liked to play practical jokes on his jailers and, in particular, he enjoyed making them drunk.' But his release was by no means certain. Would the money be raised? Could Henry VI be trusted? A song he wrote at this time reveals his state of anxiety:

'He liked to play practical jokes on his jailers'

Two pages from the *Chronicle of Petrus de Eboli*, illustrating the life of the Emperor Henry VI. In 1186, Henry married Constance, daughter of Roger II of Sicily. Three years later, when her nephew William II died, she became the heiress to the kingdom of Sicily. Henry therefore decided to march south and to conquer Sicily.

LEFT Henry VI is shown entering Rome where he forced Pope Celestine III to crown him in April 1191.

RIGHT Henry's army then invaded the kingdom of Sicily and laid siege to Naples. However, the revolt of the Welfs under Henry the Lion forced him to raise the siege and return to Germany.

Ja nus hons pris ne dira sa raison
adroitement, se dolantement non;
mes par confort puet il fere chançon.
moult ai amis, mes povre sont li don;
honte en avront, se por ma reançon
sui ces deus yvers pris.

Ce sevent bien mi honme et mi baron,
Englois, Normant, Poitevin et Gascon,
Que je n'avoie si povre conpaignon,
cui je laissasse por avoir en prixon.
je nel di pas por nul retraçon,
mes encor sui ge pris.

Ah, certes will no prisoner tell his tale
Fitly, unless as one whom woes befall,
Still, as a solace, songs may much avail:
Friends I have many, yet the gifts are small –
Shame! that because to ransom me they fail,
I've pined two years in thrall.

But all my liegemen in fair Normandy,
In England, Poitou, Gascony, know well
That not my meanest follower would I
Leave for gold's sake in prison-house to dwell;
Reproach I neither kinsman nor ally –
Yet I am still in thrall.

Philip meanwhile had been busy. Having formally defied
Richard he now felt justified in launching his armies against
Normandy. The Castellan of Gisors, Gilbert Vascœuil, opened
the gates of his castle to Philip. Gilbert's name became a byword
for treachery, but the fortress which was the key to the Vexin
and the defences of Normandy was securely in Philip's hands.
The way to Rouen was now open, but the Norman capital
was defended by one of the heroes of the Crusade, Robert
Fitzpernel, Earl of Leicester. In answer to Philip's demand that
the city be handed over to him, Robert replied that he had no
instruction from Richard to do this, but that the gates were open
and Philip could, if he cared, enter Rouen at any time. Philip
was not the man to walk into an obvious trap, but neither was
he strong enough to besiege Rouen properly, so there was
nothing left for him but to withdraw. In England, meanwhile,
troops loyal to Richard had moved up to besiege Windsor and

other castles held by John. John was on the point of capitulation when Hubert Walter arrived from Germany and suggested that a six months' truce should be made. If Richard were to be freed, a great deal of money had to be found; peace was essential. The Justiciars, naturally hesitant about taking extreme measures against a man who might one day be king, agreed at once. They then set about the mammoth task of raising the ransom. Richard wrote to them asking for a list of nobles, with the contribution of each one noted 'so that we may know how far we are bound to return thanks to each'. The Justiciars taxed England and Normandy by every method they could think of. Hostages also had to be found to satisfy Henry VI that, after Richard had been freed, the remainder of the ransom would be forthcoming. Richard gave William Longchamp the job of escorting them to Germany, but according to Gerald of Wales, this created difficulties. Traditionally noblemen's sons had to do duty as hostages, but in view of Longchamp's notorious tastes, many barons, although quite happy to see their daughters in Longchamp's hands, refused to entrust their sons to him.

'*We are bound to return thanks to each*'

Henry VI arranged to meet Philip at the end of June. Ostensibly the Emperor intended to carry out his promise to reconcile England and France, but Richard was convinced that if the two of them met he would very soon find himself in a French prison. Philip, of course, was ready to offer a great deal of money to lay his hands on Richard. Henry VI, moreover, had an urgent political problem which Philip could help him to solve. A group of princes from the Lower Rhineland, headed by the Archbishops of Mainz and Cologne, were in revolt. By allying with Philip, Henry VI would be able to attack them from two sides at once. At all costs Richard had to prevent this alliance. The prisoner became diplomat. Throughout the early summer he was busy, and eventually he succeeded in reconciling Henry VI with all the rebels of the Lower Rhineland. Owing to their vital commercial links with England, the Princes of this region were inclined to listen carefully to what Richard said. In addition, Richard promised either to persuade Henry the Lion to make peace with the Emperor, or, if the Lion proved irreconcilable, to pay an extra fifty thousand marks ransom. If this fifty thousand marks were required, Richard agreed to pay it within seven months of his release; it was now arranged that this would

185

Richard I's younger and only surviving brother, John; from a fourteenth-century manuscript.

not occur until Henry had received one hundred thousand marks. The June meeting between Henry VI and Philip did not take place. Richard had achieved his object and the Emperor had made even more political capital out of his prisoner.

When Philip heard of this treaty he sent John a message: 'Look to yourself; the devil is loosed.' John fled at once to the safety of the French Court. It was the over-hasty action of a frightened man. Not for many months yet would Richard be free. Knowing this only too well, Richard realised that peace would have to be made with King Philip. The Normans were leaderless – sheep without a shepherd, said William of Newburgh – and in no state to resist a full-scale invasion. Philip, not

186

knowing exactly when Richard would be released, was content to come to terms so that he could consolidate the gains he had already made. The first clause of the treaty made at Mantes on 9 July simply stated that Philip could keep all the lands he had taken. After his release, Richard was to pay Philip twenty thousand marks, and four more castles (including Loches) were handed over to Philip as security for this payment. Philip, of course, used the period of peace in order to prepare for war. In the hope of obtaining a fleet to invade England he formed an alliance with the King of Denmark, Cnut VI. The name Cnut interested those who knew their history; at the French Court it was taken as an omen of the impending conquest of England. The alliance was also a marriage alliance: on 15 August Philip married Ingeborg, Cnut's daughter. But on the morning after the consummation of the marriage Philip repudiated his new wife. He wished to return her to the custody of the Danish envoys who had escorted her to France, but they refused to take her back and departed in haste, leaving Ingeborg to her fate. For years Philip was to endure the condemnation of the Church rather than have the Princess of Denmark again. His dream of a new Danish invasion of England had become a domestic nightmare. But all was not yet lost – if only Henry VI could be persuaded not to release Richard. That winter, Philip and John clubbed together and decided they could afford to pay up to one hundred and fifty thousand marks to buy Richard from Henry VI; or they would pay the same sum if Henry kept Richard in prison for another year; or they would pay one thousand pounds of silver a month for as long as the Emperor cared to keep his captive.

By now Henry had received so much of the ransom money that he had fixed 17 January 1194 as the day of Richard's release. Indeed Richard, in his role as peace-maker, had become so influential a figure in imperial affairs that Henry had planned to make him King of Provence and had set 24 January as the day of Richard's coronation at Arles. This plan, if it had been carried out, would have made Richard ruler of a kingdom stretching from the Alps to the River Rhône, and including a port as important as Marseilles. Although this territory was theoretically a part of the Empire, in practice Henry VI did not have the power to impose a king over the heads of the local magnates; nor did Richard want to be distracted from his chief task, the recovery of the lost parts of Normandy. Nonetheless, from Richard's point of view the plan had its attractions. In south-west France, Richard's chief rival was the Count of Toulouse. If Richard were King of Provence as well as Duke of Aquitaine, the Count would be encircled. To a man of Richard's wide horizons the scheme was not as far-fetched as it seems at first glance; in 1198 we can find him describing himself as 'vicar of the kingdom of Arles'. But all such dreams were quickly forgotten when Philip and John put in their new bid for Richard. Henry was tempted. He postponed the date of Richard's release and summoned a meeting of the Princes of the Empire at Mainz on 2 February. Queen Eleanor was also invited to attend, as were, on the other side, the envoys sent by Philip and John. When the letters brought by those envoys were read out, Richard was much disturbed and began to despair of ever being free. Fortunately, Richard's friends among the Princes of Germany – and after his patient work of reconciliation they were many – now intervened to save him. They compelled Henry to moderate his greed and free Richard almost at once, on 4 February – but not before Henry had made one more adjustment to the terms. The ransom was definitively set at one hundred and fifty thousand marks (to match the French bid); one hundred thousand to the Emperor and fifty thousand to Leopold. And on his mother's advice, Richard resigned the kingdom of England to Henry VI in order to receive it back as a fief of the Empire. Richard was to pay his overlord five thousand marks a year. Richard was now a vassal of Philip for his Continental lands and a vassal of Henry VI for his island kingdom. But it was worth it. At long last he was a free man. On 14 March 1194, after a leisurely journey through the Low Countries, he disembarked at Sandwich. At the shrines of Canterbury and Bury St Edmunds he gave thanks for his safe return.

His freedom had been dearly bought. One hundred and fifty thousand marks was a vast sum; in weight it came to nearly thirty-four tons of silver. It was probably between two and three times as much as the King of England's total annual income. With his share of the money, Henry VI was able to fulfil his ambition and conquer Sicily.

Duke Leopold of Austria was less fortunate. For daring to imprison a Crusader he was excommunicated and ordered to pay back the ransom money. He refused. On 26 December 1194, while he was out riding, his horse fell and crushed his foot. By the next day the foot had gone black. The surgeons advised amputation but Leopold could find no one who had either the strength of mind or the heart to carry out such a painful operation. Despite Leopold's pleadings, not even his son and heir could steel himself to the task. Eventually the Duke himself had to hold an axe close to the bone of his leg and order a servant to drive the axe through with a mallet. After three blows the gangrenous foot was removed. But it was too late. On the last day of the year Leopold died, after having made his peace with the Church and promised to make full restitution to Richard. In the eyes of the English, God's justice had been done.

8 The Last War
1194-9

THERE WAS NO NEED for Richard to stay long in England. Most of the castles held in John's name capitulated hastily. The keeper of St Michael's Mount in Cornwall died of fright when he heard the news that Richard had landed. John himself lay low in Normandy. Only Nottingham offered any resistance. This was because the garrison refused to believe that Richard was in England until he took the outer gate of the castle by storm. As soon as the defenders were convinced of the identity of the man directing the siege operations, they surrendered on 28 March 1194. Then, after a day spent happily in Sherwood Forest, Richard got down to business. Men who thought they had bought their offices in 1189 were informed that, in reality, they had only leased them for a term of years, and that the term had now expired. If they wanted to remain in such lucrative positions they would have to make new financial arrangements. Plans for a comprehensive scheme of taxation were drawn up. Richard intended to recover his lost Norman possessions, and the hard-pressed English taxpayers were going to make it possible.

On 16 April, Richard stayed at St Swithin's Priory in Winchester and took a bath in order to prepare himself for the important ceremony which was to take place on the following day. This was to be a 'crown-wearing' – not a coronation, but an occasion when the King in full regalia and wearing a golden crown, walked in procession to the cathedral accompanied by all the notables of Church and State. There had not been a crown-wearing since 1158, though before that kings had been accustomed to wear their crown two or three times a year. In view of Richard's long absence and the financial burdens which he was imposing, it was thought politic to remind people of the God-given majesty of kingship.

Then with the coming of spring and the campaigning season, it was time to go to Normandy. Richard would probably have echoed the thoughts expressed by the troubadour Bertrand de Born:

PREVIOUS PAGES Effigies of Eleanor of Aquitaine and her son, Richard I, in Fontevrault Abbey.

OPPOSITE Richard I, from a chronology of the Kings of England drawn up in the fourteenth century.

I love the gay Eastertide, which brings forth leaves and flowers; and I also love the joyous songs of the birds, re-echoing through the copse. But also I love to see amidst the meadows, tents and pavilions spread; and it gives me great joy to see, drawn up on the

The justice of the King: when Richard returned to his kingdom in 1194 he had to put the country in order so that he could recover his lost Norman possessions. This illustration is taken from a twelfth-century manuscript at Dijon. Although it refers to the story of Esther, it demonstrates the need for a strong king to ensure justice in the land.

field, knights and horses in battle array; and it delights me when the scouts scatter people and herds in their path; and I love to see them followed by a great body of men-at-arms; and my heart is filled with gladness when I see strong castles besieged, and the stockades broken and overwhelmed, and the warriors on the bank, girt about by fosses, with a line of strong stakes, interlaced. ... Maces, swords, helms of different hues, shields that will be riven and shattered as soon as the fight begins; and many vassals struck down together; and the horses of the dead and the wounded roving at random. And when battle is joined let all men of good lineage think of naught but the breaking of heads and arms; for it is better to die than to be vanquished and live. I tell you, I find no such savour in food, or in wine, or in sleep, as in hearing the shout 'On! On!' from both sides, and the neighing of steeds that have lost their riders, and the cries of 'Help! Help!'; in seeing men great and small go down on the grass beyond the fosses; in seeing at last the dead, with the pennoned stumps of lances still in their sides.

Bertrand indeed had offered his services to Richard. 'I can help you. I already have a shield at my neck and a helm on my head. ... Nevertheless how can I put myself in the field without money.' Fortunately Richard had the money to keep his

194

soldiers happy. The English Exchequer worked as never before and just about managed to meet his demands. At the head of the Exchequer and supervising the whole machinery of government was Hubert Walter, now Archbishop of Canterbury. At Christmas 1193 he had been appointed Chief Justiciar. In March 1195 he was made Papal Legate. Despite the criticism voiced by those who believed that a churchman should not involve himself in worldly affairs, Hubert Walter ruled England.

No king had a better servant than he. He did for Richard what Richard's father had hoped that Thomas Becket would do for him. In terms of the great offices which he held he can

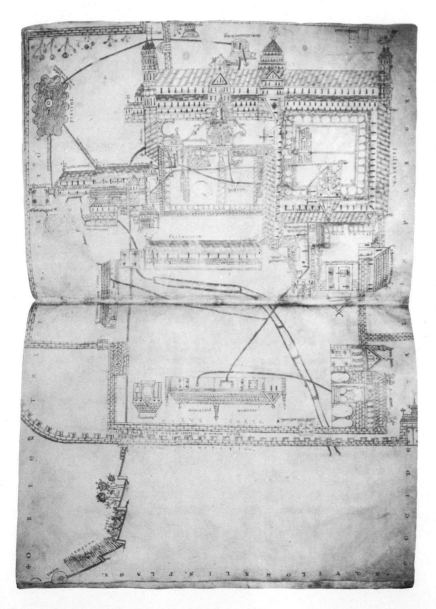

The ground plan of Canterbury Cathedral in the twelfth century. In 1174 a fire destroyed much of the eleventh-century church and it was rebuilt in the 1170s and '80s by William of Sens and William the Englishman. As can be seen in the illustration, they built in the Romanesque style, with Byzantine-style domes to the central tower and the bell towers. On the north side of the Cathedral are the monastic buildings, including the great cloisters, the infirmary and refectory, and the vineyards and fishponds.

be likened to Thomas Wolsey; in terms of his administrative genius and capacity for hard work, he compares with Thomas Cromwell. Wolsey and Cromwell – a formidable combination, and in the person of Hubert Walter the best qualities of both were united in one man. Stimulated by the pressures of a war economy, the civil service grew in size and complexity. The government wanted to do so much that it was compelled to employ the country gentry as its local agents. In the men whom Hubert Walter called in to help him we can see the distant ancestors of our Justices of the Peace. The pace of administrative development was such that it can fairly be called a revolution in government. The harvest of that revolution was the money needed to fight the war. In 1196 Hubert Walter calculated that he had supplied Richard with 1,100,000 marks in two years.

In mid-May 1194, Richard crossed the Channel to receive a tumultuous welcome when he landed at Barfleur. Old and young joined in dancing and singing: 'God has come again in his strength.' He never returned to England again. With Hubert Walter in charge there was no need to. The truce arranged in July 1193 had already been broken and Philip was besieging Verneuil. On the way to relieve Verneuil, Richard was joined by his brother John who had now decided to desert Philip. Falling to the ground at Richard's feet, John asked pardon. It was granted at once, casually and contemptuously. 'Don't be afraid, John. You are a child. You have got into bad company and it is those who have led you astray who will be punished.' But although John eventually received some of his manors back, the 'child' (he was twenty-seven in 1194) was not allowed to play with castles in England again until after Richard's death. By the end of May, Richard had cut Philip's supply line and forced him to beat a rapid retreat from Verneuil. In mid-June, he recaptured the great fortress of Loches which had been ceded to Philip in 1193. Hearing that Philip had invaded Touraine in his rear, Richard turned north again and, on 4 July, put the French army to flight at Fréteval. Richard led the pursuit; when one horse tired, he leapt astride another and rode on. He was determined to kill or capture Philip. Philip, however, left the road and hid in a church while the pursuit rolled by. So he escaped, but his camp did not. The rich booty included horses, tents, siege-engines and much of Philip's treasure. In addition,

OPPOSITE Château Gaillard, the 'saucy castle', which Richard built in 1195–8 to plug the gap in the Norman defences caused by the betrayal of Gisors. Although the castle itself was well-designed, the general collapse of Angevin power in Normandy after John's succession to the throne meant that its garrison was left in an untenable position. However, it fell to Philip Augustus after only six months of siege in 1204.

The tomb of Hubert Walter, Archbishop of Canterbury, Richard I's Chief Justiciar, in Canterbury Cathedral. The Moorish head on the left is said to represent Saladin.

OVERLEAF
Two illustrations from a twelfth-century German manuscript showing various activities of daily life. Top row, left to right: family life, shepherds, bird-catching, cooking; bottom row: farming, carpentry, artists in a monastery, priests in church.

by capturing Philip's chapel, Richard had captured the French royal archives, including documents revealing the names of those of his subjects who had been prepared to join the enemy. Despite his eagerness to hunt down the man whom he had learned to hate, Richard was still the thoughtful master tactician. His most experienced captain, William Marshal, had joined neither the pursuit nor the sack of Philip's camp, but had, on Richard's orders, held his troops together ready to deal with any attempt by the French to rally and counter-attack. That evening, as Richard's men celebrated, boasting of their great deeds and the plunder they had won, the King praised William, and, by implication, praised himself: 'The marshal did better than any of you. If there had been any trouble he would have helped us. When one has a good reserve, one does not fear one's enemies.'

The triumphant army moved south. In Poitou and Angoulême there were rebels to punish and by 22 July Richard had done this to such good effect that he was able to inform Hubert Walter that 'in these parts we have captured full 300 knights and 40,000 men-at-arms'. The letter was written from the town of Angoulême 'which we took in a single evening'.

A truce arranged by Richard's agents in Normandy now provided a year's respite from war. In order to be better prepared for the next round in the struggle Richard ordered Hubert Walter to allow tournaments to be held in England.

The Angevin Empire under Richard I

Maximum extent of Angevin Empire under Richard I

Under Richard's overlordship

Castles

Blyth
Nottingham
Stamford
Geddington
Warwick
Bury St Edmunds
Brackley
R. Thames
Oxford
Wallingford
London
Windsor
Salisbury
Westminster
Winchester
Canterbury
Dover
Portsmouth
St Michael's Mount

Boulogne
FLANDERS
BRABANT
HAINAULT
Dieppe
Barfleur
EU
Rouen
VEXIN
Louviers
Gisors
Caen
Lisieux
Château Gaillard
Evreux
CHAMPAGNE
Verneuil
Nonancourt
NORMANDY
Dreux
Paris
BLOIS
MAINE
Le Mans
Fréteval
R. Seine
ANJOU
Angers
Tours
Blois
R. Loire
Vézelay
Nantes
Fontevrault
Chinon
BURGUNDY
POITOU
TOURAINE
Issoudun
Loches
Poitiers
BERRI
La Rochelle
Lusignan
SAINTONGE
LA MARCHE
ANGOUMOIS
Limoges
Lyons
Angoulême
Chalus
LIMOUSIN
AUVERGNE
PERIGORD
Perigueux
R. Dordogne
PROVENCE
Bordeaux
AGENAIS
Agen
R. Garonne
TOULOUSE
GASCONY
Arles
Toulouse
NAVARRE
BIGORRE
Marseilles

HOLY ROMAN EMPIRE

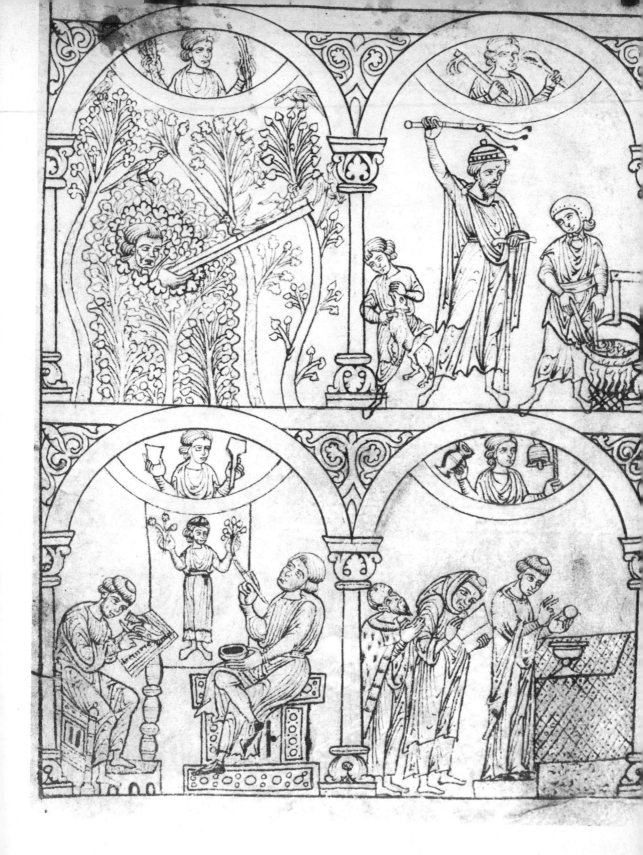

Five places, Salisbury, Stamford, Warwick, Brackley and Blyth, became licensed tournament centres. The participants had to pay entry fees ranging from twenty marks for an earl down to two marks for a landless knight. Two knights and two clerks had to be present at each official tournament, to ensure that everyone kept the peace and paid his entry fee. They were responsible to an organising committee of three earls. As Treasurer to the committee, Hubert Walter appointed his brother Theobald. It is a good illustration of the power of government in Angevin England, for Continental rulers were simply not capable of anything like this level of State control. They might allow tournaments, seeing them as good practice for war; or they might try to ban them, seeing them as a threat to public order, but they could not run them, as Richard and Hubert Walter did, as a profit-making business.

Even before leaving Germany Richard had begun to prepare for the war against Philip. He promised to pay annual pensions to a powerful group of Rhineland Princes headed by the Archbishops of Mainz and Cologne, and the Dukes of Limburg and Brabant. In return, they did homage to him against the King of

ABOVE Illustration from a twelfth-century manuscript showing activities at various times of the year. This detail shows February, and warming shoes over a fire.

RIGHT Plaster cast of Richard I's Second Great Seal.

Confirmation by Richard I to Alexander de Barentin, Butler to Henry II, of certain tenements which he had acquired. This is dated 10 November 1189 and is sealed with Richard's First Great Seal.

France. By these arrangements he laid the foundations of a system of alliances which by 1198 had effectively isolated Philip. In 1196 Richard gave the hand of his sister Joan in marriage to the new Count of Toulouse, Raymond VI. In return, Raymond agreed to send him five hundred knights for one month in the event of a war in Aquitaine. Since the King of Navarre was already Richard's brother-in-law, the treaty of 1196 meant that Richard's southern possessions were safe from attack. In 1197 the Counts of Flanders and Boulogne joined Richard's coalition. By prohibiting the export of wool and grain to Flanders, Richard had struck a damaging blow at the prosperity of the Flemish towns and so forced Count Baldwin to change sides in order to avoid economic ruin. But a gift of five thousand marks ensured that Count Baldwin was more than a reluctant ally. Richard took this form of economic warfare very seriously: when a raid upon the port of St Valery revealed the presence of some English ships in the harbour, he had the sailors hanged, the ships burned and their cargoes seized.

Soon it looked as though Richard could also count upon the spiritual power of the Papacy. In January 1198 Innocent III, the greatest of the medieval Popes, was enthroned and immediately took up the cause of Ingeborg of Denmark, the wife whom Philip had repudiated. Moreover, Innocent was delighted when Richard once again intervened in Germany. Henry VI's conquest of Sicily in 1194 meant that the Hohenstaufen had become far too powerful. They were overlords of Germany, Italy and Sicily, and the Papacy seemed to be in danger of suffocation. It therefore felt compelled to enter politics as the manager of an anti-Hohenstaufen campaign. After Henry VI's early death in September 1197, a new Emperor had to be elected and Richard decided to support the bid made by his nephew, Otto of Brunswick, in opposition to the Hohenstaufen family candidate.

Diplomatically, then, Philip was outmanœuvred and thus deprived of valuable potential aid. But castles are not captured by diplomacy alone. With Philip on the spot to organise his defences, it would not be an easy task to recover the castles and lands which the French King had overrun while Richard was in prison. And all the time, of course, Richard had to be looking to his own defences. Philip was able to use his newly-acquired

RIGHT Two illustrations from the fourteenth-century *Chroniques de St Denis.*
ABOVE The treachery of the Saracens; charitable Crusader knights are presenting alms to Saracen beggars, not suspecting that behind them are armed soldiers ready to attack.

BELOW Richard I attacking
Philip Augustus before Gisors
in 1198. Although outnumbered,
Richard charged down
upon the French army and sent
Philip Augustus flying for his life.

castles as bases from which to launch raids deep into Normandy. Richard had to repair the castles he still held and build a new one to plug the biggest gap in the Norman defences, the gap created by the betrayal of Gisors in 1193. This new castle was Richard's masterpiece: Château Gaillard, the 'saucy castle'. It was superbly sited on the rock of Andeli on a bend of the River Seine. Unfortunately the rock belonged to the Archbishop of Rouen who was reluctant to part with so valuable a site. When Richard seized it, the Archbishop replied by laying an interdict on the duchy. This meant that most church services were banned. In consequence 'the streets and squares of the cities of Normandy were littered with the unburied bodies of the dead'. Eventually the Archbishop was pacified by rich gifts of lands elsewhere, but even while the interdict was still in force Richard had begun building. Nothing was going to stop him. According to William of Newburgh the King's advisers were much alarmed when, one day in May 1198, a shower of blood fell from the sky, spattering the unfinished walls. They took it to be an evil omen. But Richard himself was unmoved and not for a moment would he allow the masons and engineers to slacken the pace of their work. 'He took such pleasure in the building that, if I am not mistaken, if an angel had descended from heaven and told him to abandon it, that angel would have been met with a volley of curses and the work would have gone on regardless.' Urged on by this unrelenting King, the whole operation – castle and adjoining fortified town – was finished within two years – by twelfth-century standards an incredibly short time. The design was based on a lifetime's experience of siege warfare in both Europe and Outremer. It incorporated the latest techniques, such as overhanging machicolated stone parapets which enabled the defenders to cover the vulnerable area at the base of the walls and towers without having to lean far out and expose themselves to the besiegers' fire. Previously, the same effect had been achieved by building a wooden gallery round the top of the tower – but wood was vulnerable to fire, particularly to the Greek Fire which we can find being used in Western Europe in the 1190s. The cost, as recorded in the documents of the Norman Exchequer, was about £11,500. Richard was well-pleased with his work. He called it his 'beautiful castle of the rock' and boasted that it was so perfectly designed that

LEFT Innocent III, who succeeded to the throne of St Peter in January 1198. He attacked Philip Augustus for repudiating the hapless Ingeborg of Denmark and supported Richard I in his struggle with the French King. Portrait from a mosaic in the Villa Catena.

pres henry le secund regna Richard sun fiz. x. aun
de my s lentre payz and de la tere seynt fuist pris del dul
de Ostriz par eyde del roy phylippe de Fraunce. e fuist reynt h
de prison pur cent mil lyueres de argent. e pur cel tauncum t
cerent les chalitz de Engletere pus. des Eglyses e venduz. p
fuist tret de vn quarel de Ablast al chastel de Chalezun. d
cebre vers fu fet: Xpe tui calicis: predo sit preda calicis.

he could hold it even if its walls were made of butter. It became Richard's headquarters and his favourite residence during the remainder of his life.

In peace-time a castle was a residence and an administrative centre; a tower block, as it were, containing both offices and flats. In war a network of castles was an effective means of defence against an invading army. If the army besieged the castles, its rate of advance was slow; if it ignored the castles and pushed on past them, there was a danger that the garrisons would be able to cut its supply lines. Under Richard the government of Normandy was responsible for about forty-five castles. This meant heavy expenditure on building, provisioning and garrisoning. Normally each castle was administratively tied to a group of estates which were supposed to produce the food and revenue needed to maintain it, but Philip's strategy was designed to prevent this happening. Instead of a full-scale invasion of the duchy, he relied on a policy of quick raids, intending to devastate the land on which the castles depended for their survival. There was nothing remarkable about this, it was the usual way of waging war in the Middle Ages. In a twelfth-century poem, the *Chronique de la Guerre entre les Anglais et les Ecossais* some grim words on the proper conduct of war were put into the mouth of Philip, Count of Flanders,

> Thus should war be begun: such is my advice
> First destroy the land and then one's foes.

With the war continuing for year after year even the fertile Seine valley began to look as bleak as the border between England and Scotland.

Static defence was of little use against the fast-moving raider. What was needed was a standing mobile army. Inevitably, this meant that Richard relied heavily, though not exclusively, on mercenaries, full-time professional soldiers who did not return home as soon as their term of service was up, but who stayed in the field for as long as they were paid. At the core of the army was Richard's own household, his permanent retinue of knights and men-at-arms. Among the other professionals were the highly-skilled and highly-paid craftsmen who built and operated the siege engines; then there were the crossbowmen; then the Welsh whose favourite weapon was the longbow, and

OPPOSITE Two scenes from the life of Richard I taken from *Effigies regum Angliae a S. Edwardo rege et confessore ad Edwardum I*. On the left, Richard is shown languishing in prison in Germany, and on the right being mortally wounded in the shoulder by a crossbowman at Chalus.

209

Builders at work, from the thirteenth-century *Book of St Albans*. The illustration shows various tools – a line and plummet level, a plumb line and mortar bowl, a windlass and basket and a carpenter's adze.

who were often given the task of clearing the enemy out of woodland – experts in the European equivalent of jungle warfare; finally there were the *routiers*, companies of soldiers who owed no allegiance to any one country, but who sold their services to anyone who could afford them. Since Richard, like his father, could outbid all other rulers, he was able to retain the most famous companies, notably that commanded by Mercadier. In his day, Mercadier was known as the 'prince of the *routiers*'. He went on crusade with Richard and fought by his side throughout the war against Philip. In Richard's new town of Andeli there was a bridge called Makade in his honour.

Richard's campaign in the summer of 1194 had enabled him to stabilise the situation and put an end to Philip's advance. In the following years he had to face the daunting task of regaining territory in an age when military technology gave most of the advantages to the defending side. Inevitably, recovery was a slow, piecemeal business. Raid was followed by counter-raid, siege by siege, conference by conference, truce by truce. In this wearisome war of attrition, Philip was a competent commander. As a director of siege operations he was probably Richard's equal. As the leader of a raiding party he knew how to inflict the maximum damage. And throughout the war he had the advantage of interior lines of communication. But he was afraid to meet Richard in pitched battle. Rather than risk defeat, and possible capture or death, he would retreat and re-open negotiations. Thus, when Richard came within striking distance of Philip's forces, he was usually able to gain ground. In November 1195, for example, Richard was at Vaudreuil in Normandy, when he learned that Philip had invaded Berri. Moving with tremendous speed he came up with Philip's army while the French king was besieging Issoudun. Philip at once sued for peace and after some weeks of negotiations the Treaty of Louviers was drawn up in January 1196. From Richard's point of view the terms of this treaty were much more favourable than the truce of 1194 had been.

This pattern was repeated in September 1198. Philip was informed that one of his castles, Courcelles-lès-Gisors in the Vexin, was in trouble and he marched to its relief. Richard had only a small fraction of his army with him, and was outnumbered. Nonetheless, he saw an opportunity to attack and knew that if he waited for reinforcements Philip would have time to see the danger. Ignoring the advice of some of the more cautious members of his household, Richard took the risk. He knew his enemy. When Richard charged down upon the French, 'like a hungry lion upon its prey', Philip took one look, turned and rode for his life. With Richard at his heels, Philip headed for the safety of Gisors. In their anxiety to get away, so many of the French knights crowded onto the bridge at the gate of Gisors that it collapsed under their weight. Philip fell into the river and had to be dragged out by his legs. At least twenty of his knights were less fortunate – they were drowned. Many more were captured, together with their horses and armour. In an exultant letter, Richard claimed a personal success. He had unhorsed three knights with a single lance. 'Thus have we defeated the king of France at Gisors. Yet it is not we who have done this but God, for we are fighting in a just cause.'

So, once again, Richard was able to make some gains when a papal legate intervened in the interests of peace and a future Crusade. It was agreed that each side should hold what it actually occupied at that moment and on this basis a five years' truce was negotiated. On 13 January 1199, the two Kings met to ratify the truce. But such was the personal bitterness between them that even now they kept their distance. Richard stayed in a boat on the Seine while Philip sat on horseback on the river bank.

Richard then went to visit Poitou while his agents negotiated what was intended to be a permanent peace, based upon a marriage alliance between Philip's son Louis and Richard's niece, Blanche of Castile. It looked as though the Angevin Empire had weathered the storm of Philip's onslaught and had come through more or less intact. Slowly but surely the gains which Philip had made in 1193 had been eroded. With his defences in first-rate order, it was now Richard who held the initiative. Undoubtedly war taxation had been a great and continuous burden on Richard's English subjects. Nonetheless the hundred years between 1150 and 1250 were years of economic growth, of rapid growth even, and there is no evidence to show that the 1190s marked an exception to the general trend. In Normandy the strains of war had been more intense and the Church, in particular, was anxious for peace. Peace did not come and John was soon to lose control of the situation. Although by no means untalented, as a commander whom men trusted, John was simply not in Richard's class. In the words of the biographer of William Marshal, 'the Normans in the old days were grain, but now they are chaff; for since the death of King Richard they have had no leadership'. With Richard gone, the Normans were blown about by every puff of wind from France. If Richard had lived, there might have been peace – the peace which would have allowed Normandy to recover from the ravages of war. Certainly there would have been better leadership. As things turned out, however, by 1204 the whole of Normandy was in Philip's hands. Even Château Gaillard fell less than five years after its builder had died.

The end came unexpectedly. A peasant in the Limousin found some buried treasure and took it to his lord, Achard of Chalus. Richard heard about this and decided that by rights the whole of the treasure should be his. In March 1199 he besieged the little castle of Chalus. According to the local story, the garrison consisted of no more than fifteen men, and they were poorly armed. One soldier – a crossbowman – had to make do with a frying-pan for a shield. At some stage, Achard offered to surrender the castle if he and his men were allowed to leave and take their arms with them. But Richard was inexorable. He swore that he would take Chalus by storm and hang them all. It was just a question of finding the weakest point in the castle's inadequate defences and sending the assault in. Richard and Mercadier rode up to take a close look. It was an affair of no importance and Richard was casual, careless. A crossbow bolt struck him in the left shoulder. Richard rode back to his quarters, making light of his wound and ordering Mercadier to press on with the attack. Chalus soon fell and all the defenders were hanged, except one – the crossbowman with the frying pan, the man who had shot Richard.

Meanwhile, Mercadier's doctor attended the King, but it proved difficult to remove the iron arrow-head. In the last few years, Richard had put on weight and the bolt had penetrated deeply. He was badly hacked about by the doctor's knife. Gangrene set in and after a few days Richard knew that he was dying. He wrote to his mother, who was at Fontevrault, asking her to come to him. So far as we know, he did not write to Berengaria. He designated John as the heir to all his dominions, and bequeathed to him three-quarters of his treasure. One-quarter was to be distributed among his servants and the poor. He then ordered the crossbowman to be brought before him. 'What harm have I done to you that you should kill me?' And the man – his name is not known with any certainty – replied, 'With your own hand you killed my father and two brothers, and you intended to kill me. Take your revenge in any way you like. Now that I have seen you on your deathbed I shall gladly endure any torment you may devise.' Upon this, Richard ordered him to be released and forgave him. But Mercadier detained the man, and after Richard's death, he had him flayed alive and then hanged.

On 6 April, eleven days after receiving his wound, Richard made his confession and then received communion – according to one chronicler, for the first time for nearly seven years. Until

'*Take your revenge in any way you like*'

213

now he had not dared to, 'because in his heart he bore a mortal hatred for the King of France'. He then received the last rites of the Church and, in the evening of that day, he died. He was forty-one years old.

Richard had been King for less than a decade. His father, Henry II, enjoys a great reputation as the King who founded the English Common Law and did much to strengthen the position of the Crown. But most of the reforms on which his reputation rests came in the second and third decades of his reign. If he had died in 1164, after a reign as short as Richard's, he would have done very little to make him famous. Most kings needed time to establish themselves – but not Richard. Within two or three years of his coming to the throne, his Crusade had already made him world-famous. Naturally he hoped to complete the task he had begun. Immediately after his release from prison he had sent an envoy to Henry of Champagne in the Holy Land. Richard's message was that he would return as soon as he could, as soon as God had given him peace and vengeance on his enemies. By 1199, the war against Philip had reached the point at which he could, at last, begin to think of returning. Jerusalem was still in Muslim hands but now that Saladin was dead and his kinsmen were fighting among themselves there was a chance that it might be recovered. There was never a Crusader-King who was Richard's equal as a general and diplomat combined. If anyone could do it, he could. It was not to be. Richard risked his life once too often. Of all kings he was the king most anxious to wage the war which his contemporaries regarded as the greatest of all wars. Yet he died in the most trivial of wars.

How are we to judge such a man? What – so far as is possible – we must not do is judge him by our standards. He was a twelfth-century Christian prince and it is by the standards expected of a man in that position that we must assess, for example, the killing of the Acre garrison. (We may also observe that in 1291 when Acre was recaptured by the Muslims the Christian population of the city was killed in revenge for the slaughter of 1192.) We may think that the Crusades were a terrible waste of human life and that the time and effort spent on these barbarous and intolerant wars could have been much better employed. But in the twelfth and thirteenth centuries even the best

OPPOSITE A page from the fourteenth-century *Chronicle of Kings*, showing: (top row, left to right) Henry II and Richard I; (bottom row) John and Henry III. (A detail of this is reproduced in colour on page 196.)

Hen. Secundus

Joħes Rex   Henricus III

educated and most humane Christians thought otherwise. The least a nobleman could do was avoid the disgrace of losing his patrimony – the lands which he inherited from his father – and the highest duty he could perform was to go on Crusade, to attempt to recover the Holy Land, the patrimony of Christ. 'If I forget thee, O Jerusalem, may my right hand forget her cunning.' By the standards of his own day Richard was right to spend his reign fighting for the Angevin Empire and for Jerusalem. Yet when he had no heir worthy to succeed him he went carelessly to Chalus.

There is an account of a conversation between two men who, in their different ways, had cause to know Richard well. In the autumn of 1192 Hubert Walter went on pilgrimage to Jerusalem and there he met Saladin. They discussed Richard. Hubert Walter praised his excellent qualities at some length, emphasising in particular his courage and his generosity. In these respects there was not a knight in the world who was his equal. Saladin listened patiently and at last replied: 'I have long since been aware that your king is a man of honour and very brave, but he is imprudent, indeed absurdly so, in the way he plunges into the midst of danger and in his reckless indifference to his own safety. For my own part, however powerful a king I might be, I would like to have wisdom and moderation rather than an excessive boldness.'

It is clear then that there were contemporaries who were capable of a realistic appraisal of Richard's character. But we should also remember that it was precisely the way he plunged into the midst of danger which made Richard something more than a competent king and a prudent general. Men might criticise Richard's 'excessive boldness'; yet it was undeniably exciting and at times, despite their own better judgement, it moved them to admiration. Most men judged Richard with their hearts as well as with their minds. For this reason it is appropriate to end, not with the cool and objective words attributed to Saladin, but with the moving lament composed by the troubadour Gaucelem Faidit:

'Your king is a man of honour and very brave'

Fortz chausa es que tot lo major dan
e-l major dol, las! q'ieu anc mais agues,
e so don dei totztemps plaigner ploran,
m'aven a dir en chantan, e retraire –
Car cel q'era de valor caps e paire,
lo rics valens Richartz, reis dels Engles,
es mortz – Ai Dieus! cals perd'e cals dans es!
cant estrains motz, e cant greus ad auzir!
Ben a dur cor totz hom q'o pot sofrir …

Ai! Seigner Dieus! vos q'etz vers perdonaire,
vers Dieus, vers hom, vera vida, merces!
Perdonatz li, que ops e cocha l'es,
e no gardetz, Seigner, al sieu faillir,
e membre vos cum vos anet servir.

I must tell and recount in song the greatest misfortune and
sorrow that, alas, I have ever known and which, henceforth,
I shall always regret and lament … for the head and father of
valour, the courageous and powerful king of the English,
Richard, is dead. Alas! oh God! what a great loss and what
pity! What a harsh word and how painful it is to hear it. The
man who can endure this pain, must, indeed, have a hard heart.

Ah! Lord God! You who art merciful, true God, true man and
the true life, have mercy! Pardon him, for he has great need of
your compassion. Do not consider his sins, but remember how
he was going to serve you!

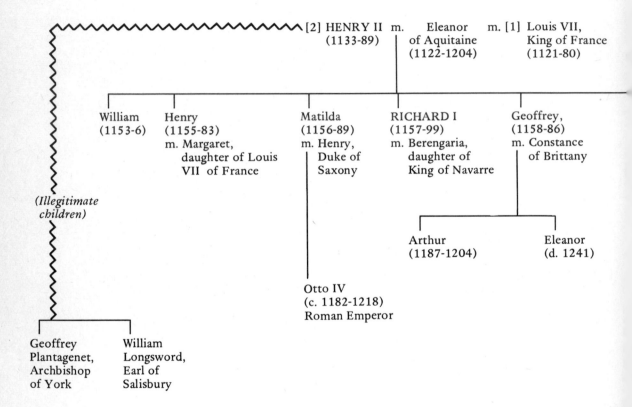

[2] HENRY II m.   Eleanor   m. [1] Louis VII,
(1133-89)   of Aquitaine   King of France
                  (1122-1204)   (1121-80)

William   Henry   Matilda   RICHARD I   Geoffrey,
(1153-6)   (1155-83)   (1156-89)   (1157-99)   (1158-86)
                 m. Margaret,   m. Henry,   m. Berengaria,   m. Constance
                    daughter of Louis   Duke of   daughter of   of Brittany
                    VII of France   Saxony   King of Navarre

(Illegitimate
children)

                                                         Arthur   Eleanor
                                                         (1187-1204)   (d. 1241)

                                       Otto IV
                                       (c. 1182-1218)
                                       Roman Emperor

Geoffrey   William
Plantagenet,   Longsword,
Archbishop   Earl of
of York   Salisbury

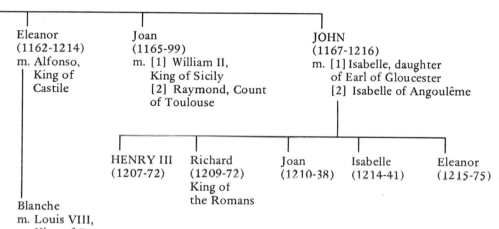

Eleanor
(1162-1214)
m. Alfonso,
   King of
   Castile

Blanche
m. Louis VIII,
   King of France

Joan
(1165-99)
m. [1] William II,
   King of Sicily
   [2] Raymond, Count
   of Toulouse

JOHN
(1167-1216)
m. [1] Isabelle, daughter
   of Earl of Gloucester
   [2] Isabelle of Angoulême

HENRY III
(1207-72)

Richard
(1209-72)
King of
the Romans

Joan
(1210-38)

Isabelle
(1214-41)

Eleanor
(1215-75)

Select bibliography

The standard biography of Richard (though now almost unobtainable) is:

    K. Norgate, *Richard the Lion Heart* (1924)

Biographies of other important figures include:

    S. Painter, *William Marshal* (1933); A. Kelly, *Eleanor of Aquitaine and the Four Kings* (1952); W. L. Warren, *King John* (1961); J. T. Appleby, *Henry II* (1962); C. R. Cheney, *Hubert Walter* (1967)

There is a very readable account of the quarrels of the Angevins in:

    A. Duggan, *Devil's Brood* (1957)

For a useful survey of events in England during Richard's reign see: J. T. Appleby, *England without Richard 1189-1199* (1965)

The history of the years 1189 to 1192 is described in:

    The Chronicle of Richard of Devizes, edited and translated by J. T. Appleby (1963)

On the Crusades see:

    H. E. Mayer, *The Crusades* (1972); S. Runciman, *A History of the Crusades*, 3 vols. (1951–54); R. C. Smail, *Crusading Warfare* (1956); B. Lewis, *The Assassins* (1967); M. J. Hubert and J. La Monte, *The Crusade of Richard Lion-heart* (1941) is a translation of Ambroise's *Estoire de la Guerre Sainte* and is the only contemporary account of the Crusade to be available in a modern and reliable English translation.

There are some fascinating passages translated from Arab sources in:

    F. Gabrieli, *Arab Historians of the Crusades* (1969)

On Sicily in this period:

    J. J. Norwich, *The Kingdom in the Sun 1130-1194* (1970)

For the conquest of Cyprus:

    Sir George Hill, *A History of Cyprus*, Vol. 1 (1940)

The standard work on the war in Normandy is:

    Sir Maurice Powicke, *The Loss of Normandy*, 2nd edn. (1961)

On twelfth-century anti-Semitism:

    M. D. Anderson, *A Saint at the Stake* (1964)

On the organisation of English society in this period:

    A. L. Poole, *Obligations of Society in the Twelfth and Thirteenth Centuries* (1946); D. M. Stenton, *English Society in the Early Middle Ages 1066-1307* (1951); F. Barlow, *The Feudal Kingdom of England 1042-1216* (1955)

Index